T0219849

Build Android-Based Smart Applications

Using Rules Engines, NLP and Automation Frameworks

Chinmoy Mukherjee

Apress®

Build Android-Based Smart Applications

Chinmoy Mukherjee
Bangalore, Karnataka, India

ISBN-13 (pbk): 978-1-4842-3326-9   ISBN-13 (electronic): 978-1-4842-3327-6
https://doi.org/10.1007/978-1-4842-3327-6

Library of Congress Control Number: 2017963550

Cover image by Freepik (www.freepik.com)

Managing Director: Welmoed Spahr
Editorial Director: Todd Green
Acquisitions Editor: Celestin John Suresh
Development Editor: Matthew Moodie
Technical Reviewer: Jojo John Moolayil
Coordinating Editor: Divya Modi
Copy Editor: April Rondeau

Distributed to the book trade worldwide by Springer Science+Business Media New York, 233 Spring Street, 6th Floor, New York, NY 10013. Phone 1-800-SPRINGER, fax (201) 348-4505, email orders-ny@springer-sbm.com, or visit www.springeronline.com. Apress Media, LLC is a California LLC and the sole member (owner) is Springer Science + Business Media Finance Inc (SSBM Finance Inc). SSBM Finance Inc is a **Delaware** corporation.

For information on translations, please email rights@apress.com, or visit http://www.apress.com/rights-permissions.

Apress titles may be purchased in bulk for academic, corporate, or promotional use. eBook versions and licenses are also available for most titles. For more information, reference our Print and eBook Bulk Sales web page at http://www.apress.com/bulk-sales.

Any source code or other supplementary material referenced by the author in this book is available to readers on GitHub via the book's product page, located at www.apress.com/978-1-4842-3326-9. For more detailed information, please visit http://www.apress.com/source-code.

Printed on acid-free paper

Table of Contents

About the Author

Chinmoy Mukherjee has worked in the software industry for the past 17 years in India, Canada, the United States, and Australia. He has written more than 100,000 lines of code and worked on 17 software projects as an "individual contributor" for 12 companies (Motorola, HP, Infineon, Cisco, etc.). He holds few interesting patents, new smartphone design, locating anonymous objects, etc. He has published many international papers on Smart application to solve "healthcare delivery" issue for developing countries, information security, and other topics. By writing this book, he wants to help 30+ million software developers to shift gears from traditional application development to smart application development. Please feel free to contact him at http://www.linkedin.com/in/chinmoym.

About the Technical Reviewer

Jojo Moolayil is an artificial intelligence professional and published author of the book *Smarter Decisions: The Intersection of IoT and Decision Science*. With over five years of industrial experience in AI, machine learning, decision science, and IoT, he has worked with industry leaders on high-impact and critical projects across multiple verticals. He is currently working with General Electric, the pioneer and leader in data science for industrial IoT, and lives in Bengaluru—the Silicon Valley of India.

He was born and raised in Pune, India, and graduated from the University of Pune with a major in information technology engineering. He started his career with Mu Sigma Inc.—the world's largest pure-play analytics provider—and then Flutura, an IoT analytics startup, and has worked with the leaders of many Fortune 50 clients.

In his present role with General Electric, he focuses on solving AI and decision-science problems for industrial IoT use cases as well as on developing data-science products and platforms for industrial IoT.

Apart from authoring books on decision science and IoT, Jojo has also been technical reviewer for various books on machine learning and business analytics with Apress. He is an active data-science tutor and maintains a blog at http://www.jojomoolayil.com/web/blog/.

You can reach out to Jojo at:

- `http://www.jojomoolayil.com/`

- `https://www.linkedin.com/in/jojo62000`

I would like to thank my family, friends, and mentors for their kind support and constant motivation throughout my life.

—Jojo John Moolayil

Acknowledgments

Examples available at rules engines websites are modified as required, and the modified code snippets are provided. Thanks to Abhishek Chander (Bachelor of Computer Science Cambridge University) for developing the AutoQuiz prototype under the guidance of author Chinmoy Mukherjee.

Introduction

This book describes how to build smart applications using cutting-edge technologies like rules engines, code automation frameworks, and natural language processing (NLP).

Note A smart application is an application embedded with intelligence. The intelligence can be updated on the fly.

This book provides step-by-step guidance on porting nine rules engines (CLIPS, JRuleEngine, DTrules, Zilonis, Termware, Roolie, OpenRules, JxBRE, and JEOPS) to the mobile platform. Then, it describes how to use each rules engine to build a smart application. Sample code snippets are provided so that the reader can get started with programming their smart application immediately. The book also describes porting issues with other popular rules engines (Drools, JLisa, Take, Jess, and OpenRules).

This book will guide the reader on how to automatically generate an working smart application based on requirement specifications.

This book concludes with showing the reader how to generate a smart application from unstructured knowledge using the NLP framework Stanford POS (part of speech) tagger.

PART I

Rules Engines

CHAPTER 1

Which Rules Engine Is Best for Building Smart Applications?

Let us now evaluate rules engines based on agility, scalability, and usability and decide which is best suited for developing smart applications. We'll start by defining what a rules engine is.

Rules engines help embed intelligence into an application. The intelligence can be updated on the fly. Readers should be aware of programming calculators. Rules engines can be thought of as much more sophisticated versions of such calculators. CLIPS can be downloaded from Source Forge [24].

```
java -jar CLIPSJNI.jar
CLIPS> (+ 3 4)
7
CLIPS> (defglobal ?*x* = 3)
CLIPS> ?*x*
3
CLIPS> red
red
CLIPS> (bind ?a 5)
5
```

3

© Chinmoy Mukherjee 2018
C. Mukherjee, *Build Android-Based Smart Applications*,
https://doi.org/10.1007/978-1-4842-3327-6_1

```
CLIPS> (+ ?a 3)
8
CLIPS> (reset)
CLIPS> ?a
[EVALUATN1] Variable a is unbound
FALSE
CLIPS>
```

Sample code is taken from [23]. There are diverse types of rules engines written in Java that vary widely in functionality and concept. The revenue from business rules engines exceeded $460 million in 2011 [1]. The total market size for the mobile application market will be as big as $25 billion by 2015 [2]. As per Gartner, developing context-aware mobile applications is one of the top trends [3].

Mobile applications are becoming increasingly complex. This is making way for rules engines on mobile platforms. Rules engines can help keep business logic separate from application logic. At this point in time, not many rules engines are known to work on mobile platforms. We have ported and evaluated nine rules engines: CLIPS, OpenRules, JXBRE, JEOPS, Roolie, Termware, JRuleEngine, Zilonis, and DTRules in Android. This chapter provides a detailed description, step-by-step porting guides, and sample working code for each of the rules engines. We also discuss the issues faced while attempting to port other popular rules engines, like Drools, JLisa, "Take," and Jess. We compared the rules engines based on licensing, language used to develop, rules syntax, reasoning method, multi-threading support, scalability, and so on in Android [4]. If you are trying to use a rules engine in a mobility project, this chapter can save more than four staff weeks of effort.

What Is a Rules Engine?

A rules engine is software that executes one or more rules in a runtime production environment, and each rules engine has its own proprietary rule-storage formats with varying features. Today, rules engines are used in domains such as finance, healthcare, retail, manufacturing, and so on.

Rules engines are becoming increasingly popular for the following reasons:

- Separation of business logic from application

- Rules can be managed separately from application code.

- Ease of writing rules for domain experts

Rules engines allow more flexibility in applications. Applications can be rolled out much faster using rules engines. Other advantages include understandable rules, tool integration, speed, scalability, and declarative programming.

Android has become the number one mobile platform (Figure 1-1) [5]. As the need for context-aware intelligent applications grows, rules engines are bound to be integrated into more and more Android applications.

The main contribution of this chapter is the evaluation of nine rules engines on the Android platform. This chapter describes each of the rules engines in detail and provides a summary of each. Nine rules engines are evaluated and compared against each other for various aspects like license, language, rules, reasoning, multi-threading support, scalability, and so on. The chapter concludes with our recommendation about the rules engine best suited for Android platform.

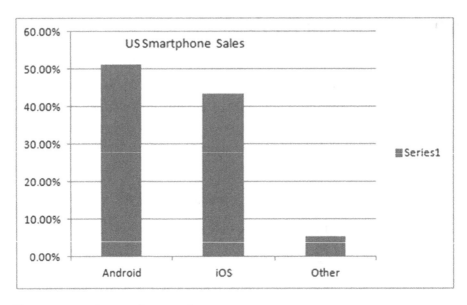

Figure 1-1. *Smartphone sales*

CLIPS

CLIPS [6] is a rules engine written in C language. It is the most widely used rules engine as it is fast and free.

It is portable and can easily be integrated with software written in C, Java, FORTRAN, and ADA. Wide varieties of complex knowledge can be represented using CLIPS rules. The software is available in the public domain, making it the choice of the industry. Here is a summary of the rules engine (Figure 1-2).

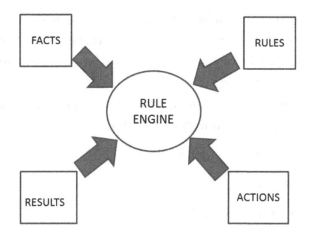

Figure 1-2. *CLIPS rules engine*

- License type: Public domain

- Language: C

- Works on Android: Yes

- Rules Syntax: Lisp-like

- Memory Footprint: 0.83 MB

- Reasoning Method: Rete [22]

- Supports multi-threading: No

- Easy to scale the rules engine: Yes, with average time to run being 17.4 milliseconds

JRuleEngine

JRuleEngine [7] is a Java-based rules engine that employs a forward-chaining algorithm and is designed as per JSR 94 specifications. Rules are defined in an XML file.

There are two kinds of rules. One is a stateful rules session that remembers the state of facts and can be queried repetitively. The other is a stateless rules session, which gives good performance but does not remember the state of facts.

The rules engine uses a set of input objects and generates a set of output objects. Here is a summary of the rules engine:

- License type: Open source, LGPL

- Language: Java

- Works on Android: Yes

- Rules Syntax: Condition-action pattern

- Memory Footprint: 0.062660217 MB

- Reasoning Method: Forward-chaining algorithm

- Supports multi-threading: Yes

- Easy to scale the rules engine: Yes, with average time to run being 0.24163 seconds

DTrules

DTrules [8] is a Java-based high-performance rules engine.

Rules are in the form of decision tables, which provide a simple way to describe logic in a tabular form. Unbalanced decision tables are supported, which reduces the effort required to build them. DTRules can be easily integrated into Java applications.

It supports domain-specific language (DSL). It has a small memory footprint. Here is a summary of the rules engine:

- License type: Open source (Apache 2.0 Open Source License)

- Language: Java

- Works on Android: Yes

- Rules Syntax: Decision table

- Memory Footprint: 0.540092468 MB

- Reasoning Method: Uses a structured set of data and a set of decision Tables to implement policy rules

- Supports multi-threading: Yes

- Easy to scale the rules engine: No

Zilonis

Zilonis [9] is a multi-threaded rules engine. It is based on a variation of the forward-chaining Rete algorithm. Its rules representation language is similar to LISP. It also provides a scripting environment for Java-based applications.

Here is a summary of the rules engine:

- License type: GPL

- Language: Java

- Works on Android: Yes

- Rules Syntax: Similar to Lisp

- Memory Footprint: 0.683494568 MB

- Reasoning Method: A variation of the forward-chaining Rete algorithm

- Supports multi-threading: Yes

- Easy to scale the rules engine in cloud: Yes, with average time to run being 0.65863 seconds

Termware

Termware [9] is a rule-processing framework that can be easily embedded in Java applications. It has a formal semantic model based on the concept of a term system with actions. It allows extreme flexibility in applications for high adaptability to a changeable environment, easy re-engineering, and component reuse. Here is a summary of the rules engine:

- License type: Other

- Language: Java

- Works on Android: Yes

- Rules Syntax: Proprietary

- Memory Footprint: 0.195205688 MB

- Reasoning Method: One object, many patterns matching approach

- Supports multi-threading: Yes

- Easy to scale the rules engine: Yes, with average time to run being 11.3892 seconds.

Roolie

Roolie [11] is an extremely simple Java rules engine. It is a non-JSR 94 rule engine designed particularly to use rules created in Java. Basic rules are written in separate Java files and are chained together in an XML file to create more-complex rules. Here is a summary of the rules engine:

- License type: Open source LGPL

- Language: Java

- Works on Android: Yes

- Rules Syntax: XML

- Memory Footprint: 0.594 MB (608 KB)

- Reasoning Method: Proprietary

- Supports multi-threading: No

- Easy to scale the rules engine: Yes, with average time to run being 2.87 seconds

OpenRules

OpenRules [12] is a business decision management system (BDMS) that provides rules-based application development. It works in a simple Java "OpenRules" API or the standard JSR-94 interface. It is used to create decision support systems that can be used to create, execute, and maintain business rules in applications. Rules are specified in Excel files in the form of decision tables, removing the learning part for its users as it just requires familiarity with MS Excel. It allows you to change the business rules/logic in the Excel sheet at runtime without the need to deploy it again. It supports parallelism, enabling it to work in multi-threaded environments. Figure 1-3 depicts the OpenRules workflow.

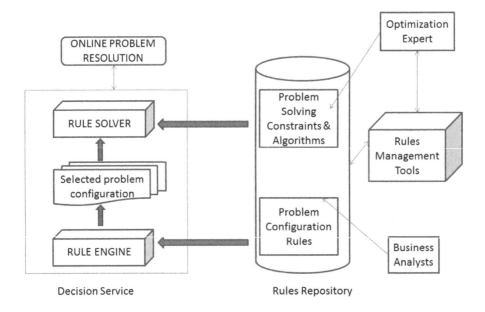

Figure 1-3. *OpenRules rules engine*

Here is a summary of the rules engine:

- License type: Both open source (GPL) and commercial (Non-GPL)

- Language: Java

- Works on Android: Yes

- Rules Syntax: Decision tables in Excel files

- Memory Footprint: 2 MB

- Reasoning Method: Proprietary

- Supports multi-threading: Yes

- Easy to scale the rules engine: No

JxBRE

JxBRE [13] is a lightweight Java-based business rules engine (BRE). Rules are written in an XML file along with logic defining the flow of the application based on the execution of rules. It is both a forward-chaining, data-driven inference engine and an XML-driven flow-control engine. Here is a summary of the rules engine:

- License type: GPL

- Language: Java

- Works on Android: Yes

- Rules Syntax: XML

- Memory Footprint: 1.44 MB (1474 KB)

- Reasoning Method: Proprietary

- Supports multi-threading: No

- Easy to scale the rules engine: Yes, with average time to run being 2.57 seconds

JEOPS

JEOPS [14] is a Java-based rules engine for embedding forward-chaining production rules into Java applications. It provides artificial intelligence capabilities to the application.

JEOPS production rules can be written in a text file (.rules file). The interaction with the knowledge base is performed by four methods, Tell (object), Flush (), Retract (object), and Modified (object). The time required for Java programmers to learn JEOPS is minimized by its using Java expressions in the rule definitions. Here is a summary of the rules engine:

- License type: Open Source LGPL

- Language: Java

- Works on Android: Yes

- Rules Syntax: "Condition-action" patterns in any text editor

- Memory Footprint: 0.03 MB (31.5 KB)

- Reasoning Method: RETE

- Supports multi-threading: No

- Easy to scale the rules engine: Yes, with average time to run being 120ms

CHAPTER 2

Steps to Port Rules Engines

This chapter will cover how to port major rules engines in android platform.

CLIPS

Android-ndk and Eclipse Helios were used to port CLIPS into Android. It is better to use a Linux machine for porting. Here are the steps to port CLIPS into Android:

- Download CLIPSJNI source code from Source Forge and build an Android library project from the source code.

  - Export the library project to `CLIPSJNI.jar`.

- Create a dummy Android project and create a JNI directory under your project directory.

- Copy all source (*.c) and header (*.h) files from CLIPS to JNI directory.

- Add all source files *except main.c* in `Android.mk`.

© Chinmoy Mukherjee 2018
C. Mukherjee, *Build Android-Based Smart Applications*,
https://doi.org/10.1007/978-1-4842-3327-6_2

- Your Android.mk should look like the following:

```
LOCAL_PATH := $(call my-dir)
include $(CLEAR_VARS)
LOCAL_MODULE    := CLIPSJNI
LOCAL_SRC_FILES := agenda.c \
analysis.c \
argacces.c \
.
.
.
CLIPSJNI_Environment.c
LOCAL_LDLIBS    := -lm -llog -ljnigraphics
include $(BUILD_SHARED_LIBRARY)
```

- Search for setlocale function in JNI directory.
  Wherever setlocale is expected to return a value,
  hardcode it to C and comment out all other setlocale
  calls, as Android's setlocale returns a hard-coded 0!

- Comment out main function (just to be on the safe
  side).

- Run ndk-build –b.

- Copy libCLIPSJNI.so to libs/armeabi and libs/
  armeabi-v7a.

- Add CLIPSJNI.jar to your Android project as an
  external jar.

JRuleEngine

Here are the steps to port JRuleEngine into Android:

- Download jsr172.jar.

  - Remove all packages from this jar file except java.rmi.

- Repackage the jar using jarjar.jar utility as follows:

  - Create rulefile.txt containing the following line: rule java.rmi.** com.<yourcompany>.java.rmi.@1.

  - On command prompt, run java -jar jarjar.jar process rulefile.txt <input jar> <output jar>.

- Download jsr94-1.1.jar.

- Repackage the jar using jarjar.jar utility.

  - Create a rulefile.txt file containing the following line: rule java.rmi.** com.<yourcompany>. java.rmi.@1.

  - On command prompt, run: java -jar jarjar.jar process rulesfile.txt <input jar> <output jar>.

- Download Apache Harmony awt.jar and remove all java.* packages from the jar.

- Download jruleengine.jar with source code.

- Comment all the else if statements containing a Component.getName() function call; also remove the import java.awt.Component; statement.

- Repackage `jruleengine.jar` using jarjar.jar utility.

- Create `rulefile.txt` file containing the following rule:

  - `rule java.rmi.** com.<yourcompany>.java.`
    `rmi.@1 rulejava.awt.Component**org.apache.`
    `harmony.awt.ComponentInternals@1`

  - `run java -jar jarjar.jar process rulefile.txt`
    `<input jar> <output jar>`

- Create an Android project and add all these jars to the build path of the project.

- Copy XML file containing rules to sdcard in emulator.

DTrules

The jar files work in Android but the following steps need to be executed to use DTrules in Android applications:

- Write rules as decision tables in an Excel sheet. Sample Excel sheets are available at `sampleprojects/<projectname>/DecisionTables`.

- Create a file structure as follows:

  ```
  /DecisionTables/excel_sheet_containing_decision_
  tables.xls
  /edd/file_containing_edd.xls
  /xml/
  /DTRules.xml
  ```

- Convert Excel sheet containing rules to XML by using code like the following:

  ```
  Excel2XML.compile("root path", "DTRules.xml",
  "name_of_ruleset", "path_to_repository");
  ```

- To generate the mapping file automatically, use something like this:

```
String [] maps = {"main" };
Excel2XML.compile(path,"DTRules.xml",
"<rule name>","D:/XLS2XML/repository",maps);
```

- Create an Android project.

- Add the following jars to the build path: `java-cup-11a.jar`, `poi-3.6-20091214.jar`, `dtrules.jar`.

- Create a mapping file (if not generated automatically) to map XML file with data into the entities.

- Add the required entities to the initialization section, which needs to be pushed to the entity stack before the first decision table is executed. As an example:

```
<initialization>
<initialentity entity="constants" epush="true" />
<initialentity entity="job" epush="true" />
<initialentity entity="value" epush="true" />
</initialization>
```

- Modify the number of each entity required to be created. For example:

```
<entities>
  <entity name="constants" number="1" />
  <entity name="job" number="1" />
  <entity name="value" number="1" />
</entities>
```

- Create a file structure in sdcard as follows:

  - `/sdcard/xml/mapping_file.xml,edd_file.xml,dt_file.xml`

  - `/sdcard/repository/DTRules.xml`

  - `/sdcard/DTRules.xml`

  - `/sdcard/testfiles/testcase.xml`

- Copy the generated files into appropriate directory of sdcard.

Zilonis

Zilonis jar works in Android without any issue. Here are the steps to add Zilonis into your Android project:

- Create an Android project.

- Copy the .clp file containing rules into a folder, say the temp folder in sdcard in emulator.

- Add `zilonis0.97b.jar` and `antlr.jar` to the project's build path.

While writing rules files (.clp) for Zilonis, please ensure the following:

- In .clp file, only one statement can be added in one line, unlike CLIPS.

- No space should be between lines.

Termware

Porting Termware in Android was easy. Here is the one step:

- Remove all debug stub-related items from Java files belonging to ua.gradsoft.termware and ua.gradsoft. termware.util in the TermWare.jar.

Roolie

No effort was required to port Roolie onto Android—you just need to add the jar file to the Android project and get going.

OpenRules

- Download the source code for org.apache.commons. beanutils, recompile it, and export it to jar after removing the following packages, to fix multiple definition issues:

  org.apache.commons.logging
  org.apache.commons.logging.impl

- Then, repackage it using the jarjar.jar utility:

  - Create rulefile.txt containing the following rule: rule java.beans.** com.googlecode. openbeans.@1

  - Run the following command in command prompt to repackage: java -jar jarjar-1.4.jar process rulefile.txt <input jar> <output jar>

- Download `poi-3.6-20091214.jar` for Excel-sheet processing.

- Download `openbeans-1.0.jar` for using `com.googlecode.openbeans`, as OpenRules uses Java beans extensively, which is not supported by Android.

- Download `commons-lang-2.3.jar` and remove the `org.apache.commons.lang.enum` package, then recompile it.

- Create an Android project and add all these jars to the build path of the project.

- OpenRules seems to have hard coded the path of `openrules.config dir`, in which template files need to be stored. Create a directory `openrules.config` under sdcard and put the rule and template files there.

JxBRE

The following steps need to be followed to port JXBRE into Android:

- Download the source code of Xerces 1.4.4 (XML Parser).

- Change the name of package `javax` to anything else.

- Recompile the source code and build the project.

- Export it to jar file `xerces.jar`.

- Download `jxbre.jar` and `ideaityUtil.jar`.

- Create an Android project and add all these jars to the build path of the project.

- Download the XML Schema file `businessRules.xsd`.

- Copy the rule file (.xml) and `businessRules.xsd` into emulator, from which it can be accessed in the project.

JEOPS

JEOPS can be ported into Android as follows:

- Create a new Java project.

- Add the JavaBean file (declaring the variables being used and their accessor methods) to it. Compile it and copy the `.class` file from bin.

- Create a new directory and paste the `.class` file just generated there in appropriate folders according to the package name specified in the `.class` file.

- Also, copy the rule-base file (.rules) to this directory.

- Download JEOPS.jar and put it in the directory.

- In command prompt, go to the location/path of this new directory and execute the following command to generate a Java file from the rule-base file:

  ```
  java -cp JEOPS.jar;. jeops.compiler.Main <rule file>
  ```

- Create an Android project and add the generated rule-base java file in the project.

- Create a new jar with the JavaBean `.java` file (by compiling it and exporting it to jar) and add it to the build path of your Android project.

- Add the following lines to the code of the rule-base Java
  file for accessing tell():

```
_knowledgeBase.tell(f1);
_knowledgeBase.tell(f2);
private jeops.AbstractKnowledgeBase _knowledgeBase;
_knowledgeBase = knowledgeBase;
```

- Also add JEOPS.jar to the build path of your project.

Sample Code Snippet

This code snippet will help you understand how to integrate a rules engine
with an Android application.

CLIPS

Let's build a smart application using the CLIPS rule engine to assess
diarrhea symptoms for a patient.

Figure 2-1 shows what the app looks like.

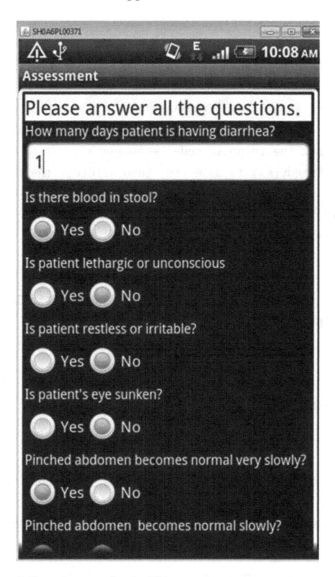

Figure 2-1. *What the app looks like*

The diarrhea guideline can be easily codified in CLIPS as diarrhoea.clp.

```
;=======================================
;;
;; ---- DIARRHEA MANAGEMENT------
;;
;=======================================
;=======================================
;--- Printout the response code---
;; If the Remedy(Rx) is asserted, then printout the remedy.
;=======================================
        (defrule print_diarrhea_message2
        (Rx_diarrhea_signs_code(code ?b))

   =>

      (bind ?*WHODecisionCode* (create$ ?*WHODecisionCode* ?b))
        ;(printout t ?*WHODecisionCode* crlf)

        )

;; RULES FOR ASSESSMENT OF PATIENT STATE AND TRIGGER THE
DIARRHEA MANAGEMENT

;=======================================
;--- Check if the patient has diarrhea ---
;; If the patient data has (diarrhea yes) then (check blood in
stool) and (classify dehydration)
;; If the patient data has (diarrhea no) then (check other disease)
;=======================================

(defrule check-diarrhea_yes
        (diarrhea_data (diarrhea yes))  ;; Check if the patient
        has diarrhea
   =>
```

```
        (assert (check blood_in_stool))           ;; TRIGGER
        CHECK BLOOD IN STOOL
        (assert (classify dehydration)))          ;; TRIGGER
        CLASSIFY DEHYDRATION
;;----------------------------------------------------------------
;;----------------------------------------------------------------
(defrule check-diarrhea_no
        (diarrhea_data (diarrhea no))
  =>
        (assert (check other disease)) )
;=======================================
;--- Rule check blood in stool ---
;; If the patient has (blood in stool) then the patient state
is (dysentery).
;=======================================
 (defrule check-blood_in_stool-yes
         (check blood_in_stool)
        ;; check if the action is triggered from the diarrhea
         (diarrhea_data (blood_in_stool yes))
         ;; check if the patient has blood in stool
  =>
         (assert (Rx_diarrhea_signs_code (code "10"))))
         ;; ASSERT THE Decision Code : 1 which means dysentry
;=======================================
;--- Rule check blood in stool ---
;; If the patient has (no blood in stool) then the patient
state is (no dysentery).
;=======================================
```

```
 (defrule check-blood_in_stool-no
        (check blood_in_stool)
        ;; Check if the action is triggered from the diarrhea rule system
        (diarrhea_data (blood_in_stool no))
        ;; Check if the patient has no blood in stool
=>)                        ;; END THE ASSESSMENT OF DYSENTERY

;=======================================
;--- Assess Treatment Objective: Severe Dehydration ---
;=======================================
(defrule classify-severe_dehydration
        (classify dehydration)
        ;; Check if the action is triggered from the diarrhea rule system
        (diarrhea_data(blood_in_stool no))
        (diarrhea_data(severe_condition_count ?w&:(>= ?w 2)))
                        ;; If more than two of the following
                        some_dehydration signs are satisfied
        (diarrhea_data(how_many_days ?x&:(<= ?x 14)))
        ;; If diarrhea 14days or more

=>
        (assert (Rx_diarrhea_signs_code (code "5")))
        ;(assert (check-more_than_14days-severe_dehydration_case))
)

(defrule classify-severe_dehydration_child_able_to_drink
(Rx_diarrhea_signs_code (code "5"))
(diarrhea_data (not_able_to_drink_or_drinking_poorly no))
=>
        (assert (Rx_diarrhea_signs_code (code "5A")))

)
```

28

```
(defrule classify-severe_dehydration_child_not_able_to_drink
(Rx_diarrhea_signs_code (code "5"))
(diarrhea_data (not_able_to_drink_or_drinking_poorly yes))
=>
        (assert (Rx_diarrhea_signs_code (code "5B")))

)

;========================================
;--- Objective: Some Dehydration ---
;========================================
(defrule classify-some_dehydration
        (classify dehydration)
        ;; Check if the action is triggered from the diarrhea rule system
        (diarrhea_data (blood_in_stool no))
        (diarrhea_data(some_condition_count ?w&:(>= ?w 2)))
        (diarrhea_data (severe_condition_count ?y&:(< ?y 2)))
                        ;; If more than two of the following
                        some_dehydration signs are satisfied
        (diarrhea_data (how_many_days ?x&:(<= ?x 14)))
        ;; If diarrhea 14 days or more

=>

        (assert (Rx_diarrhea_signs_code (code "6")))
        ;(assert (check-more_than_14days-some_dehydration_case))
)

;;;;;;;;;;;;;;;;;;;;;;;;;;;;;;;;;;;;;;;;;;;;;;;;;;;;;;;;;;;;;;;;;;;;;;

(defrule classify-no_dehydration
        (classify dehydration)                ;; Check if the
        action is triggered from the diarrhea rule system
        (diarrhea_data (blood_in_stool no))
```

```
        (diarrhea_data (how_many_days ?x&:(<= ?x 14)))
        (diarrhea_data (severe_condition_count ?w&:(< ?w 2)))
        (diarrhea_data(some_condition_count ?y&:(< ?y 2)))
=>

        (assert (Rx_diarrhea_signs_code (code "7")))
)

;;;;;;;;;;;;;;;;;;;;;;;;;;;;;;;;;;;;;;;;;;;;;;;;;;;;;;;;;;;;;;;;;

;; RULES FOR DETERMINATION OF TREATMENT OBJECTIVES BASED ON
PATIENT'S STATE
;=======================================
;--- Rules for Assessment of Persistent Diarrhea ---
;--- Check-more_than_14days ---
;=======================================
;=======================================
;--- Rules for Check-more_than_14days - Patient is classified
to either have Severe or Some dehyration + diarrhea is >14
; then it is severe persistent diarrhea
;=======================================
(defrule check-severe_persistent_diarrhea-severe_deh_case
;(check-more_than_14days-severe_dehydration_case)
;; Check if the assessment of Persistent Diarrhea is triggered
(or (diarrhea_data (some_condition_count ?w&:(>= ?w 2)))
(diarrhea_data (severe_condition_count ?y&:(>= ?y 2))))
(diarrhea_data (how_many_days ?x&:(> ?x 14)))
(diarrhea_data (blood_in_stool no))
;; If diarrhea 14days or more
=>
(assert (Rx_diarrhea_signs_code(code "8"))) )
;; ASSERT THE TREATMENT OBJECTIVE :SEVERE PERSISTENT DIARRHEA
```

```
;========================================
;--- Rules for Check-more_than_14days - Patient has not been
classified to have dehydration but if diarrhea is >14 days then
it is persistent diarrhea
;========================================
(defrule check-persistent_diarrhea-no_deh_case
;(check-more_than_14days-no_dehydration_case)
;; Check if the assessment of Persistent Diarrhea is triggered
(diarrhea_data (some_condition_count ?y&:(< ?y 2)))
(diarrhea_data(severe_condition_count ?w&:(< ?w 2)))
(diarrhea_data(how_many_days ?x&:(> ?x 14)))
(diarrhea_data (blood_in_stool no))
;; If diarrhea 14days or more
=>
(assert (Rx_diarrhea_signs_code (code "9"))) )
;; ASSERT THE TREATMENT OBJECTIVE :PERSISTENT DIARRHEA
```

The user input can be modeled as diarrheaData:

```
public class diarrheaData  implements Parcelable {
    int iNumberofDays=0;
     String sBlood_In_Stool="no";
    String sLethargic_Unconscious="no";
     String sRestless_Irritable="no";
    String sSunken_Eyes="no";
    String sSkin_Pinch_Veryslow="no";
    String sSkin_Pinch_Slow="no";
    String sNot_Able_To_Drink_or_Drinking_Poorly="no";
    String sDrinking_Eagerly_or_Thirsty="no";
    String sOther_Severe_Disease="no";
    String sTrained_nurse_for_iv_immediately="no";
    String sIv_available_in_30min="no";
```

```
    String sTrained_nurse_for_ng_tube_immediately="no";

}
                static {
                        try {
                        System.loadLibrary("CLIPSJNI");
                        if(clips == null) {
                        clips = new Environment();
                        }
                        }
                        catch(UnsatisfiedLinkError ule) {
                        Log.e("JNI", "Could not load
                        libCLIPSJNI.so!");
                        }
                        private  static Environment clips = null;
                        static {
                        try {
                        if(clips == null) {
                        clips = new Environment();
                        }
                        clips.clear();
                        clips.load("diarrhoea.clp");
                String myassertString = "(diarrhea_data
                (diarrhea yes) " +
                "(blood_in_stool "+mydiarrheaData.sBlood_In_
                Stool +") " +
                "(how_many_days "+mydiarrheaData.
                iNumberofDays+") " +
                "(lethargic_unconscious "+mydiarrheaData.
                sLethargic_Unconscious+") "+
                "(restless_irritable "+mydiarrheaData.sRestless_
                Irritable+") " +
```

```
                    "(sunken_eyes "+ mydiarrheaData.sSunken_Eyes+") " +
                    "(skin_pinch_veryslow "+mydiarrheaData.sSkin_
                    Pinch_Veryslow+") " +
                    "(skin_pinch_slow "+mydiarrheaData.sSkin_Pinch_
                    Slow+") " +
                    "(not_able_to_drink_or_drinking_poorly "+mydiarrhea
                    Data.sNot_Able_To_Drink_or_Drinking_Poorly+") " +
                    "(drinking_eagerly_or_thirsty "+mydiarrheaData.
                    sDrinking_Eagerly_or_Thirsty+") " +
                    "(other_severe_Vdisease " + otherSevereDisease + "))";
clips.assertString(myassertString);
                         clips.run();
                         MultifieldValue mv = (MultifieldValue)
                         clips.eval("?*WHODecisionCode*");

                             String WHODecision;
List theList = mv.listValue();
for(Iterator itr = theList.iterator(); itr.hasNext();)
{
   StringValue myValue = (StringValue) itr.next();
   WHODecision = WHODecision + myValue.toString() + " ";

}
```

The decision will be available in WHODecision variable.

If the reader could understand the preceding CLIPS example, the rest of the examples will be straightforward to understand.

JRuleEngine

```
Class.forName( "org.jruleengine.RuleServiceProviderImpl" );
            String path     = Environment.getExternalStorage
            Directory().getAbsolutePath()+"/temp/example3.xml";
            InputStream inStream = new FileInputStream( new
            File(path) );
            // Get the rule service provider from the provider
            manager.
            RuleServiceProvider serviceProvider =
            RuleServiceProviderManager.getRuleServiceProvider
            ( "org.jruleengine" );
            // get the RuleAdministrator
            RuleAdministrator ruleAdministrator =
            serviceProvider.getRuleAdministrator();
            System.out.println("\nAdministration API\n");
            System.out.println( "Acquired RuleAdministrator: "
            + ruleAdministrator );
            // get an input stream to a test XML ruleset
            // This rule execution set is part of the TCK.
            //  InputStream inStream = new FileInputStream(
            "example3.xml" );
            System.out.println("Acquired InputStream to
            example3.xml: " + inStream );
            // parse the ruleset from the XML document
            RuleExecutionSet res1 = ruleAdministrator.
            getLocalRuleExecutionSetProvider(
            null ).createRuleExecutionSet( inStream, null );
            inStream.close();
            System.out.println( "Loaded RuleExecutionSet: " + res1);
```

```java
// register the RuleExecutionSet
String uri = res1.getName();
ruleAdministrator.registerRuleExecutionSet
(uri, res1, null );
System.out.println( "Bound RuleExecutionSet to
URI: " + uri);
// Get a RuleRuntime and invoke the rule engine.
System.out.println( "\nRuntime API\n" );
RuleRuntime ruleRuntime = serviceProvider.
getRuleRuntime();
System.out.println( "Acquired RuleRuntime: " +
ruleRuntime );
// create a StatefulRuleSession
StatefulRuleSession statefulRuleSession =
        (StatefulRuleSession) ruleRuntime.
        createRuleSession( uri,
        new HashMap(),
        RuleRuntime.STATEFUL_SESSION_TYPE );
System.out.println( "Got Stateful Rule Session: " +
statefulRuleSession );
// Add some clauses...
ArrayList input = new ArrayList();
input.add(new Clause("Socrate is human"));
// add an Object to the statefulRuleSession
statefulRuleSession.addObjects( input );
System.out.println( "Called addObject on Stateful
Rule Session: " + statefulRuleSession );

statefulRuleSession.executeRules();
System.out.println( "Called executeRules" );
```

```
                // extract the Objects from the statefulRuleSession
                List results = statefulRuleSession.getObjects();
                System.out.println( "Result of calling getObjects: " +
                                    results.size() + " results." );
                // Loop over the results.
                Iterator itr = results.iterator();
                while(itr.hasNext()) {
                        Object obj = itr.next();
                        System.out.println("Clause Found: "+obj.
                        toString());
                }
                // release the statefulRuleSession
                statefulRuleSession.release();
                System.out.println( "Released Stateful Rule Session." );
```

DTrules

```
String path = Environment.getExternalStorageDirectory().
getAbsolutePath()+"/";
String decisionTable = "Compute_Eligibility";
//String decisionTable = "Calculate Individual Income";
RulesDirectory rd = new RulesDirectory(
path,
"DTRules.xml");
RuleSet rs = rd.getRuleSet("KidAid");
IRSession session;
try {
Excel2XML.compile(path,"DTRules.xml","KidAid","sdcard");
session = rs.newSession();
Mapping mapping = session.getMapping();
mapping.loadData(session, path+"testfiles/"+"TestCase_001.xml");
```

```java
session.execute(decisionTable);
printReport(session, System.out);
} catch (RulesException e) {
// TODO Auto-generated catch block
e.printStackTrace();
} catch (Exception e) {
// TODO Auto-generated catch block
e.printStackTrace();
}
}
```

Zilonis

```java
String fileName = "YOUR RULE FILE";
FileInputStream fstream = new FileInputStream(fileName);
int lineCount = getLines(fileName);
System.out.println("line is "+ lineCount);
DataInputStream dis = new DataInputStream(fstream);
BufferedReader br = new BufferedReader(new
InputStreamReader(dis));
ZilonisLexer lexer = new ZilonisLexer(dis);
ZilonisParser parser = new ZilonisParser(lexer);
GenericEventHandler geh = new GenericEventHandler(rete);
parser.setEventHandler(geh);
try {
while(lineCount-- > 0) {
parser.statement();
}
} catch (RecognitionException e) {
// TODO Auto-generated catch block
e.printStackTrace();
```

```
} catch (TokenStreamException e) {
// TODO Auto-generated catch block
e.printStackTrace();
}
} catch (FileNotFoundException e3) {
// TODO Auto-generated catch block
e3.printStackTrace();
} catch (IOException e) {
// TODO Auto-generated catch block
e3.printStackTrace();
}
```

Termware

```
String[] args = {"iReduce"};
TermWare.getInstance().init(args);
ITermRewritingStrategy strategy=new FirstTopStrategy();
IFacts facts=new DefaultFacts();
TermSystem termSystem=new TermSystem(strategy,facts,TermWare.
getInstance());
termSystem.addRule("x->y");
termSystem.addRule("y->z");
Term inputTerm=TermWare.getInstance().getTermFactory().
createAtom("x");
Term outputTerm=termSystem.reduce(inputTerm);
if(outputTerm.getName().equals("z")){
Log.d("iReduce Termware","success");
}
}}catch(TermWareException ex){
Log.e("iReduce Termware", "eror:"+ex.getMessage());
ex.printStackTrace();
}}
```

38

Roolie

```
public class AbdominalRuleArgs extends RuleArgs{
        public enum ArgField
        {
        User
        , right_lower_abdomen
        , left_lower_abdomen
        , pain_nausea
        , blood_in_stool
        , blood_in_urine
        };
        public String getUser()
        {
        return getString(ArgField.User);
        }
        public void setUser(String user)
        {
        setString(ArgField.User, user);
        }
        }
        public abstract class AbdominalRule implements Rule{
        @Override
        public boolean passes(RuleArgs ruleArgs) {
        // TODO Auto-generated method stub
        if (false == (ruleArgs instanceof AbdominalRuleArgs))
        {
        Log.msg("ruleArgs must be an instance of
        AbdominalRuleArgs ");
        return false;
        }
```

```
// Cast RuleArgs to AbdominalRuleArgs and validate
AbdominalRuleArgs abArgs = (AbdominalRuleArgs) ruleArgs;
// Muse have all args set
if (false == abArgs.isright_lower_abdomenSet()
|| false == abArgs.isleft_lower_abdomenSet()
|| false == abArgs.isUserSet()
|| false == abArgs.ispain_nauseaSet()
|| false == abArgs.isblood_in_stoolSet()
|| false == abArgs.isblood_in_urineSet()
)
{
Log.msg("Not all the arguments in AbdominalRuleArgs are set.");
return false;
}
// If all args are there, let the child class do its
evaluation
return passes(abArgs);
}
public void onCreate(Bundle savedInstanceState) {
      super.onCreate(savedInstanceState);
   // Get the config file as an InputStream
   InputStream is =
            Main.class.getClassLoader().
            getResourceAsStream(
      "roolie/abdominal/roolie-config.xml");
   RulesEngine rules = new RulesEngine(is);
   // Create some rule arguments (aka "Facts") to test
   for some users
   List<AbdominalRuleArgs> abdominalRuleArgsList =
   createRuleArgsToTest();
   // See if rules pass for each BankingRuleArgs created.
   for (AbdominalRuleArgs ruleArgs : abdominalRuleArgsList)
```

```
        {
          msg("\n* Evaluating " + ruleArgs.getUser()+"'s
          health:\n");
          boolean isUltrasound =rules.passesRule("Ultrasound",
          ruleArgs);
          boolean isCTScan =rules.passesRule("CTScan", ruleArgs);
          boolean isStoolTest1 =rules.
          passesRule("StoolTest1", ruleArgs);
          boolean isStoolTest2 =rules.
          passesRule("StoolTest2", ruleArgs);
          boolean isStoolTest3 =rules.
          passesRule("StoolTest3", ruleArgs);
          boolean isNothing =rules.passesRule("NoTest",
          ruleArgs);
        }
}
```

OpenRules

```
UserInput userInput=new UserInput("no","yes","yes","no","yes");
            Response response=new Response();
            String fileName = "file:sdcard/openrules.
            config/DecisionOneOrTwo.xls";
            Decision decision = new Decision("DecisionAbdom
            inalPain",fileName);
            decision.put("userInput", userInput);
            decision.put("response", response);
            decision.execute();
public class UserInput {
        String right_lower_abdomen;
        String left_lower_abdomen;
        String pain_nausea;
```

```java
        String blood_in_stool;
        String blood_in_urine;
        public UserInput(String rla,String lla,String pn,String
        bis,String biu){
                this.right_lower_abdomen =rla;
                this.left_lower_abdomen =lla;
                this.pain_nausea =pn;
                this.blood_in_stool =bis;
                this.blood_in_urine =biu;
        }
        public String getRight_lower_abdomen() {
                return right_lower_abdomen;
        }
        public void setRight_lower_abdomen(String right_lower_
        abdomen) {
                this.right_lower_abdomen = right_lower_abdomen;
        }
public class Response {
        String comment;
        public Response(){
                this.comment="Helllllp";
        }
        public String getComment() {
                return comment;
        }
        public void setComment(String s) {
                comment = s;
        }
```

```java
String[] products;
/**
 * @return
 */
public String[] getProducts() {
        if (products == null)
                products = new String[0];
        return products;
}
/**
 * @param strings
 */
public void setProducts(String[] strings) {
        products = strings;
}
public String toString() {
        StringBuffer buf = new StringBuffer(2500);
        buf.append("Offered Products:").append("\n");
        for (int i = 0; i < getProducts().length; ++i) {
                buf.append("\t").append(getProducts()
                [i]).append("\n");
        }
        if (comment != null)
                buf.append("Comment: ").append
                (comment).append("\n");

        return buf.toString();
}
}
```

JxBRE

```java
public void onCreate(Bundle savedInstanceState) {
        super.onCreate(savedInstanceState);
        bre = new BREImpl();
        args=new String[]{ "/data/data/" +packageName +"/files/
        abdominal.xml"};
        //args="-s D:\\android_training\\rules\\discount.xml";
        setContentView(R.layout.main);
        copyCLPFiles("abdominal.xml");
        copyCLPFiles("businessRules.xsd");
        AbdominalMainLoad(args);
          Inputs order = new Inputs();
          getTotal(order);
                }
    private void copyCLPFiles(String fileName) {
                try {
                        File file = getFileStreamPath(fileName);
                        if(file.exists()) {
                                return;
                        }
                        else  {
                                InputStream myInput =
                                getAssets().open(fileName);
                                OutputStream myOutput = new
                                FileOutputStream(
                                        "/data/data/" +
                                        getPackageName() +"/
                                        files/"+fileName);
                                //transfer bytes from the
                                inputfile to the outputfile
                                byte[] buffer = new byte[1024];
```

```java
        int length;
        while ((length = myInput.
        read(buffer))>0){
                myOutput.write(buffer,
                0, length);
        }
        //Close the streams
        myOutput.flush();
        myOutput.close();
        myInput.close();
    }
}
catch (FileNotFoundException e) {
        e.printStackTrace();
} catch (IOException e) {
        e.printStackTrace();
}
}
public void AbdominalMainLoad(String[] args) {
    try {
            Document doc = loadFile(args[0]);
            // Let's register as a listener....
            ((BREImpl)bre).addListener(this);
            ((BREImpl)bre).init(doc);
    }
    catch (Exception e) {
            System.err.println("Could not create
             document");
            e.printStackTrace();
    }
}
```

```java
/**
* Let's pretend that we have an Object called Order and
it has all
* relevant order information including an Object for
the Product that
* is ordered
*/
public void getTotal(Inputs aOrder) {
        // Have to do this so the anonymous classes can
        get to it..
        inp = aOrder;
        BRERuleContext aBRC = bre.getRuleContext();
        /**
        * This is the best way to do this. Better than
        wrapper classes.
        * Don't know why I didn't think of this earlier....
        */
        aBRC.setFactory(BLOOD_IN_URINE, new
        BRERuleFactory() {
                public Object executeRule(BRERuleContext
                aBrc, Map aMap, Object aStep) {
                        return inp.getBlood_in_urine();
                }
        });
        aBRC.setFactory(BLOOD_IN_STOOL, new
        BRERuleFactory() {
                public Object executeRule
                (BRERuleContext aBrc, Map aMap, Object
                aStep) {
                        return inp.getBlood_in_stool();
                }
        });
```

```
aBRC.setFactory(RIGHT_LOWER_ABDOMEN, new
BRERuleFactory() {
        public Object
        executeRule(BRERuleContext aBrc, Map
        aMap, Object aStep) {
                return inp.getRight_lower_
                abdomen();
        }
});
aBRC.setFactory(LEFT_LOWER_ABDOMEN, new
BRERuleFactory() {
        public Object executeRule(BRERuleContext
        aBrc, Map aMap, Object aStep) {
                return inp.getLeft_lower_abdomen();
        }
});
aBRC.setFactory(PAIN_NAUSEA, new BRERuleFactory() {
        public Object executeRule(BRERuleContext
        aBrc, Map aMap, Object aStep) {
                return inp.getPain_nausea();
        }
});
aBRC.setFactory(RECCTEST_BLOODURINE, new
BRERuleFactory() {
        public Object executeRule(BRERuleContext
        aBrc, Map aMap, Object aStep) {
                return DecisionString.getDecis
                ionString( new String((String)
                aMap.get(TEST1)) );
        }
});
```

```
aBRC.setFactory(RECCTEST_RIGHTLOWER, new
BRERuleFactory() {
        public Object executeRule(BRERuleContext
        aBrc, Map aMap, Object aStep) {
                return DecisionString.getDecision
                String( new String((String)
                aMap.get(TEST2)) );
        }
});
aBRC.setFactory(RECCTEST_LEFTLOWER, new
BRERuleFactory() {
        public Object executeRule(BRERuleContext
        aBrc, Map aMap, Object aStep) {
                return DecisionString.getDecis
                ionString( new String((String)
                aMap.get(TEST3)) );
        }
});
aBRC.setFactory(NOTHING, new BRERuleFactory() {
        public Object executeRule(BRERuleContext
        aBrc, Map aMap, Object aStep) {
                return DecisionString.get
                DecisionString( new String
                ((String)aMap.get(TEST4)) );
        }
});
//bre.process();
bre.process("SET1");
bre.process("SET2");
bre.process("SET3");
bre.process("SET4");
```

```
//System.out.println(bre.getRuleContext().
toString());
if ((aBRC.getResult(RECCTEST_
BLOODURINE))!=null) {
System.out.println((String)aBRC.
getResult(RECCTEST_BLOODURINE).getResult());
}
else {}
if ((aBRC.getResult(RECCTEST_
RIGHTLOWER))!=null) {
System.out.println((String)aBRC.getResult(RECCTEST_
RIGHTLOWER).getResult());
}
else {}
if ((aBRC.getResult(RECCTEST_LEFTLOWER))!=null)
{
        System.out.println(aBRC.getResult
        (RECCTEST_LEFTLOWER).getResult());
}
else {}
if (aBRC.getResult(NOTHING)!=null) {
        System.out.println(aBRC.getResult
        (NOTHING).getResult());
}
else {}
}
```

JEOPS

```java
for(int i=0; i <100; i++) {
    Fibonacci f = new Fibonacci(i);
 FibonacciBase kb = new FibonacciBase(new
PriorityConflictSet());
 kb.tell(f);
 kb.run();
 System.out.println(f.getN() + "the number of the fibonacci
series = " + f.getValue());
}
```

CHAPTER 3

Issues Faced While Porting Rules Engines

We found a few issues while trying to write rules in each of the following rules engines. The reader should make a note of these issues.

- Jruleengine: It does not support OR operator.

- Zilonis: It doesn't support OR, defglobal, or bind keywords, unlike CLIPS.

- DTRules: The facts have to be provided in an XML file, so running rules in an environment where facts have to be provided at runtime is complex and tedious.

- Termware: Rules have to be written in code itself.

- Roolie: Too many rules files need to be developed, and each rule needs to be coded in a separate Java file.

- JxBRE: ElseIf doesn't work in XML files (we can use Set instead). Only one If works in the logic part of the rules file (.xml). Any one of {Rule, Log, Logic, While, InvokeSet, ForEach, Retract} is expected before an If element.

© Chinmoy Mukherjee 2018
C. Mukherjee, *Build Android-Based Smart Applications*,
https://doi.org/10.1007/978-1-4842-3327-6_3

- JEOPS: The variables used as arguments for calling a function need to be initialized in rules file itself (by calling appropriate setter method).

- OpenRules: There is no document/readme explaining how to write rules.

Porting Issues for Other Rules Engines

The reader might face the following issues when porting other rules engines:

- Drools: Eclipse runs out of memory (500 MB) while converting it to dalvik format. Increasing the memory of Eclipse did not solve the issue. The reader may try to use high-end machine (RAM > 4 GB).

- JLisa: While running in Android, it throws a stack overflow issue. Reader may contact JLisa support for a resolution.

- Take: Need Java compiler at runtime. Reader may contact Take support for Android compiler support.

- Jess: Development license costs around $15,000 (US).

- OpenRules:

  - Method `org.apache.poi.hssf.usermodel.` `HSSFSheet.autoSizeColumn` in `poi-3.6-20091214.` `jar` uses class `java.awt.font.FontRenderContext`, which is not available in Android.

  - Method `com.googlecode.openbeans.` `StandardBeanInfo.getIcon` uses class `java.awt.` `image`, which is not available in Android.

- While processing decisions, garbage collection runs multiple times, indicating huge memory usage.

- Did not receive any response from the company OpenRules about the type of commercial license supported and the cost of the license.

CHAPTER 4

Comparison of Rules Engines for Mobile Platforms

This chapter contains a comparison of rules engines used for developing on mobile platforms.

Summarizing the Rules Engines

Out of all nine rules engines evaluated for Android, CLIPS is undoubtedly the most elegant, as it is fastest, free, and supports its own rules programming language. It is followed by OpenRules, where rules can be easily written in an Excel sheet, then by JEOPS, since algorithms can be easily represented. Next would be Termware, since integrating rules with your application is straightforward. Because of its portability, extensibility, and low cost, CLIPS has been widely used by governments, private enterprises, and universities. CLIPS has enabled the embedding of artificial intelligence into a wide range of applications in diverse computing environments.

Comparison of Rules Engines

Table 4-1 shows a comparison of the rules engines.

55

© Chinmoy Mukherjee 2018
C. Mukherjee, *Build Android-Based Smart Applications*,
https://doi.org/10.1007/978-1-4842-3327-6_4

Table 4-1. *A Comparison of the Rules Engines in This Book*

Rules Engine	License	Language	Rules Syntax	Memory	Reasoning	Multi-Threading	Scalability	Rating (1 to 5)
CLIPS	Public Domain	C	LISP like	83 MB	Rete	No	Yes	4
Jruleengine	LGPL	Java	*condition-action* patterns	.03 MB	Rete	No	Yes	3
DTRules	Apache 2.0	Java	Excel sheet	.54 MB	Proprietary	Yes	No	4
Zilionis	GPL	Java	CLIPS	.68 MB	Rete	Yes	Yes	3
Termware	Special	Java	Java	.19 MB	Pattern Matching	Yes	Yes	4
Roolie	LGPL	Java	XML	.59 MB	Proprietary	No	Yes	3
OpenRules	GPL/Commercial GPL	Java	Excel sheet	2 MB	Proprietary	Yes	No	4
JxBRE	GPL	Java	XML	1.44 MB	Proprietary	No	Yes	3
JEOPS	LGPL	Java	*condition-action* patterns	.03 MB	Rete	No	Yes	4

CHAPTER 5

Requirements and Challenges Faced in Knowledge Application Development

Knowledge management is defined as creating, sharing, using, and managing information for a system or organization.

In this chapter, we will discuss the requirements, challenges, design, and implementation of two knowledge management systems: SmartAppGen and AutoQuiz.

Introducing SmartAppGen and AutoQuiz

SmartAppGen automatically generates the corresponding knowledge application from structured knowledge represented as XML, Excel sheets, PPT, and so forth. For example, suppose a health worker needs to undergo training for a few weeks. At the training, they have to go through hundreds of pages of knowledge materials. What if a knowledge application is automatically built using the knowledge available and

57

© Chinmoy Mukherjee 2018
C. Mukherjee, *Build Android-Based Smart Applications*,
https://doi.org/10.1007/978-1-4842-3327-6_5

then installed on their smartphone? The training time could be reduced drastically; also, the health worker would not have to remember hundreds of pages of documentation. They would not have to refer to the printed guidelines from time to time to execute their daily routine. So, it is clear that knowledge application can increase the efficiency and accuracy of healthcare services.

Not all knowledge is so well formatted that a knowledge application can be automatically developed and installed on a smartphone. So, people would still have to undergo training and remember the things learned at training. AutoQuiz comes in handy in cases where knowledge (for instance, training materials, presentations, and so on) is given in a text format. It can generate a meaningful quiz from the unstructured knowledge. At the end of any training or presentation, a quiz can be automatically generated, and all participants can be asked to take the quiz. Then, their scores are immediately calculated. This achieves three things: people would be more alert in training, the trainer would get immediate feedback on the effectiveness of their training, and the trainer/manager would know which people were falling short in understanding and take appropriate measures to bring them up to the mark. This chapter will help with automating the knowledge management of your company or institute.

Developing Knowledge Applications

To design, develop, and deploy a knowledge application, the steps shown in Figure 5-1 are executed.

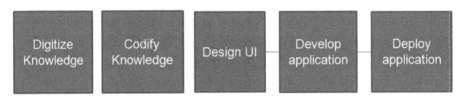

Figure 5-1. *Knowledge application development*

Here are the main requirements and challenges associated with a knowledge application:

- Representing knowledge in a digitized format and converting it into rules is a cumbersome and time-consuming process.

- The user interface can vary based on user profile. For example, a user interface can be text based for tech savvy, icon based for semi-literate, or voice based for illiterate users.

- Data persistence and maintenance is cumbersome and if not managed properly may result in application outage.

- The same application may need to be developed for multiple mobile phone platforms; e.g., Android, iOS, and so forth.

- Common features get implemented again and again in such mobile applications, wasting thousands of development hours.

- Multiple languages may need to be supported.

- Application installable may need to be customized based on user profile.

- Upgrading knowledge application should be feasible over the air.

Let us see in the next chapter how SmartAppGen can automatically generate a knowledge application. We will also address the challenges faced by knowledge application developers.

PART II

SmartAppGen: Automatically Generate Knowledge Application from Structured Knowledge

CHAPTER 6

Design and Implementation of SmartAppGen

SmartAppGen is a set of frameworks to help generate knowledge-based applications from structured knowledge automatically. Structured knowledge can be provided in various formats, like an Excel sheet, text, and XML.

- Questions, rules, information, and so forth are extracted from the document and saved as XML.

- From the generated XML(s), the corresponding Android layout, Android activity, CLIPS rules, and decision engine are generated.

- Various frameworks, like speech-to-text, audio capturer, photo capturer, upload manager, and so forth are also automatically embedded into the project.

- Generated code frameworks are glued together to generate a full-fledged Android project from a new Android project.

© Chinmoy Mukherjee 2018
C. Mukherjee, *Build Android-Based Smart Applications*,
https://doi.org/10.1007/978-1-4842-3327-6_6

CHAPTER 7

Architecture of SmartAppGen

We came up with a three-tier high-level and low-level architecture for SmartAppGen. See Figure 7-1.

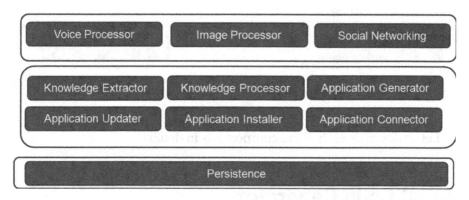

Figure 7-1. *High-level SmartAppGen architecture*

A complex knowledge application needs to support social networking, image and voice processing, over-the-air upgrade capabilities, and persistence-management functionalities. So, SmartAppGen must be able to generate such functionalities.

© Chinmoy Mukherjee 2018
C. Mukherjee, *Build Android-Based Smart Applications*,
https://doi.org/10.1007/978-1-4842-3327-6_7

Based on the application workflow, we came up with a low-level architecture for SmartAppGen.

Figure 7-2 describes all components of SmartAppGen present in the presentation, application, and data tiers.

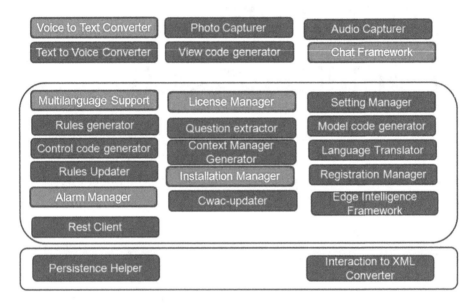

Figure 7-2. *Low-level architecture*

Let us describe each of the components in detail.

Model Code Generator

This framework generates the code representing the model for the knowledge/guideline (e.g., GuidelineData.java).

View Code Generator

This framework generates the user interface code (e.g., Guidelinescreen. java) for the knowledge/guideline.

Controller Code Generator

This framework generates the controller code for the knowledge guideline (e.g., Mainactivity.java).

Question Extractor

This block extracts the guideline type (decisive/informative), questions, answer types, and answer values and builds question.xml automatically.

Context Manager Generator

This framework generates a context manager corresponding to the knowledge application.

Rules Generator

This framework converts the digitized guidelines to rules. For each guideline, a set of rules files are generated. In the DTRules rules engine, decisions are represented in an Excel sheet. Excel2XML converts decisions to XML files that are processed by the rules engine. In CLIPS, a rules header can easily be generated from the registration information and questions. The developer would have to just codify the remaining part of the rules.

Language Translator

This framework provides support for translating the application text into multiple languages.

Persistence Helper

This framework will help with persisting the application data to a local database.

Interaction to XML Converter

This framework converts the user interactions (e.g., model) to XML.

Rules Upgrader

This framework will help upgrade rules over the air.

Cwac-updater

This open source framework [1] can be used to upgrade Android applications over the air.

Voice-to-Text Converter

This framework will convert a user's voice to text.

Text-to-Voice Converter

This framework will help convert text to voice and help the application interact with users via voice.

Photo Capturer

This is a generic framework to capture photos.

Audio Capturer

This is a generic framework for capturing audio for voice recording or any other purpose.

Chat Framework

This framework enables the chat functionality.

Edge Intelligence Framework

This framework needs to be built on top of the rules engine and helps the application communicate with the rules engine with ease.

REST Client

This framework will help the application make use of restful web services exposed by any JAX-RS–compliant server.

Installation Manager

This framework ensures that the appropriate components and accessories are packaged in the installable based on the profile of the user.

CHAPTER 8

Example of Generating Knowledge Application from Knowledge

Figure 8-1 represents knowledge from which one can derive a list of medical tests a patient needs to undergo based on the symptoms of the patient.

© Chinmoy Mukherjee 2018
C. Mukherjee, *Build Android-Based Smart Applications*,
https://doi.org/10.1007/978-1-4842-3327-6_8

Chief Complaint - Chest Pain					
Symtoms		EKG	Blood Tests/ Blood Oxygen Level	No Tes	chest x-ray
Does the pain occur with exertion?		yes			
Does the pain radiate to the neck, jaw, and/or arms?		yes			
Does the pain have a "squeezing" or "tightness" quality?		yes			
Can the pain be reproduced by movement of the arms or torso or by pushing on a certain area of the chest?		No			yes
Is the pain made worse by deep breathing?		No			yes
Is the pain brought on by eating or lying down? Is it relieved with antacids?		No		yes	
Is it accompanied by shortness of breath, sweating, a feeling of "clamminess," nausea or indigestion?		yes			
If the pain is anginal in nature, does it last more than 15 to 30 minutes?		yes			

Figure 8-1. *Knowledge in Excel sheet*

From the Excel sheet depicted in Figure 8-1, corresponding Android layout and CLIPS rules files are generated.

Android Layout Corresponding to Knowledge

The Android layout XML is provided here for the sake of completeness.

```
<?xml version="1.0" encoding="utf-8"?>
<ScrollView xmlns:android="http://schemas.android.com/apk/res/
android"
        android:layout_width="match_parent"
        android:layout_height="fill_parent">
<LinearLayout xmlns:android="http://schemas.android.com/apk/
res/android"
        android:id="@+id/com_test_DummyProject_chief_complaint_
        chest_painscreen_layout1"
        android:orientation="vertical"
        android:layout_width="fill_parent"
        android:layout_height="fill_parent">
<TextView android:text="Does the pain occur with exertion?"
android:id="@+id/com_test_DummyProject_chief_complaint_chest_
painscreen__exertion" android:layout_width="wrap_content"
android:layout_height="wrap_content">
</TextView>
<RadioGroup android:layout_width="wrap_content" android:orien
tation="horizontal" android:id="@+id/com_test_DummyProject_
chief_complaint_chest_painscreen__exertionRadioGroup1"
android:layout_height="wrap_content">
<RadioButton android:text="yes"  android:layout_height="wrap_
content" android:checked="false" android:id="@+id/com_test_
DummyProject_chief_complaint_chest_painscreen__exertion_yes"
android:layout_width="wrap_content">
</RadioButton>
```

```xml
<RadioButton android:text="no"  android:layout_height="wrap_
content" android:checked="true" android:id="@+id/com_test_
DummyProject_chief_complaint_chest_painscreen__exertion_no"
android:layout_width="wrap_content">
</RadioButton>
</RadioGroup>
<TextView android:text="Does the pain radiate to the neck,
jaw, and/or arms?" android:id="@+id/com_test_DummyProject_
chief_complaint_chest_painscreen_radiate_neck__jaw__arms"
android:layout_width="wrap_content" android:layout_
height="wrap_content">
</TextView>
<RadioGroup android:layout_width="wrap_content" android:orienta
tion="horizontal" android:id="@+id/com_test_DummyProject_chief_
complaint_chest_painscreen_radiate_neck__jaw__armsRadioGroup2"
android:layout_height="wrap_content">
<RadioButton android:text="yes"  android:layout_height="wrap_
content" android:checked="false" android:id="@+id/com_test_
DummyProject_chief_complaint_chest_painscreen_radiate_neck__
jaw__arms_yes" android:layout_width="wrap_content">
</RadioButton>
<RadioButton android:text="no"  android:layout_height="wrap_
content" android:checked="true" android:id="@+id/com_test_
DummyProject_chief_complaint_chest_painscreen_radiate_neck__
jaw__arms_no" android:layout_width="wrap_content">
</RadioButton>
</RadioGroup>
<TextView android:text="Does the pain have a squeezing or
tightness quality?" android:id="@+id/com_test_DummyProject_
chief_complaint_chest_painscreen_squeezing_tightness"
android:layout_width="wrap_content" android:layout_
height="wrap_content">
```

```
</TextView>
<RadioGroup android:layout_width="wrap_content" android:orienta
tion="horizontal" android:id="@+id/com_test_DummyProject_chief_
complaint_chest_painscreen_squeezing_tightnessRadioGroup3"
android:layout_height="wrap_content">
<RadioButton android:text="yes"  android:layout_height="wrap_
content" android:checked="false" android:id="@+id/com_test_
DummyProject_chief_complaint_chest_painscreen_squeezing_
tightness_yes" android:layout_width="wrap_content">
</RadioButton>
<RadioButton android:text="no"  android:layout_height="wrap_
content" android:checked="true" android:id="@+id/com_test_
DummyProject_chief_complaint_chest_painscreen_squeezing_
tightness_no" android:layout_width="wrap_content">
</RadioButton>
</RadioGroup>
<TextView android:text="Can the pain be reproduced by movement
of the arms or torso or by pushing on a certain area of the
chest?" android:id="@+id/com_test_DummyProject_chief_complaint_
chest_painscreen_reproduced_movement_arms_torso_pushing_area_
chest" android:layout_width="wrap_content" android:layout_
height="wrap_content">
</TextView>
<RadioGroup android:layout_width="wrap_content" android:orienta
tion="horizontal" android:id="@+id/com_test_DummyProject_chief_
complaint_chest_painscreen_reproduced_movement_arms_torso_pushing_
area_chestRadioGroup4" android:layout_height="wrap_content">
<RadioButton android:text="yes"  android:layout_height="wrap_
content" android:checked="false" android:id="@+id/
com_test_DummyProject_chief_complaint_chest_painscreen_
reproduced_movement_arms_torso_pushing_area_chest_yes"
android:layout_width="wrap_content">
</RadioButton>
```

```
<RadioButton android:text="no"  android:layout_height="wrap_
content" android:checked="true" android:id="@+id/
com_test_DummyProject_chief_complaint_chest_painscreen_
reproduced_movement_arms_torso_pushing_area_chest_no"
android:layout_width="wrap_content">
</RadioButton>
</RadioGroup>
<TextView android:text="Is the pain made worse by deep breathing?"
android:id="@+id/com_test_DummyProject_chief_complaint_chest_
painscreen_worse_deep_breathing" android:layout_width="wrap_
content" android:layout_height="wrap_content">
</TextView>
<RadioGroup android:layout_width="wrap_content" android:orienta
tion="horizontal" android:id="@+id/com_test_DummyProject_chief_
complaint_chest_painscreen_worse_deep_breathingRadioGroup5"
android:layout_height="wrap_content">
<RadioButton android:text="yes"  android:layout_height="wrap_
content" android:checked="false" android:id="@+id/com_test_
DummyProject_chief_complaint_chest_painscreen_worse_deep_
breathing_yes" android:layout_width="wrap_content">
</RadioButton>
<RadioButton android:text="no"  android:layout_height="wrap_
content" android:checked="true" android:id="@+id/com_test_
DummyProject_chief_complaint_chest_painscreen_worse_deep_
breathing_no" android:layout_width="wrap_content">
</RadioButton>
</RadioGroup>
<TextView android:text="Is the pain brought on by eating or
lying down? Is it relieved with antacids?" android:id="@+id/
com_test_DummyProject_chief_complaint_chest_painscreen_
brought_eating_lying_down__relieved_antacids" android:layout_
width="wrap_content" android:layout_height="wrap_content">
```

```
</TextView>
<RadioGroup android:layout_width="wrap_content" android:orienta
tion="horizontal" android:id="@+id/com_test_DummyProject_chief_
complaint_chest_painscreen_brought_eating_lying_down__relieved_
antacidsRadioGroup6" android:layout_height="wrap_content">
<RadioButton android:text="yes"  android:layout_height="wrap_
content" android:checked="false" android:id="@+id/
com_test_DummyProject_chief_complaint_chest_painscreen_
brought_eating_lying_down__relieved_antacids_yes"
android:layout_width="wrap_content">
</RadioButton>
<RadioButton android:text="no"  android:layout_height="wrap_
content" android:checked="true" android:id="@+id/
com_test_DummyProject_chief_complaint_chest_painscreen_
brought_eating_lying_down__relieved_antacids_no"
android:layout_width="wrap_content">
</RadioButton>
</RadioGroup>

<LinearLayout xmlns:android="http://schemas.android.com/apk/
res/android"
        android:orientation="horizontal"
        android:layout_weight="1"
        android:layout_width="fill_parent"
        android:layout_height="wrap_content">
<Button android:text="saveButton" android:layout_weight="0.5"
android:id="@+id/com_test_DummyProject_chief_complaint_chest_
painscreen_saveButton" android:layout_width="wrap_content"
android:layout_height="wrap_content"></Button>
<Button android:text="cancelButton" android:layout_weight="0.5"
android:id="@+id/com_test_DummyProject_chief_complaint_chest_
```

painscreen_cancelButton" android:layout_width=*"wrap_content"*
android:layout_height=*"wrap_content"*></Button>

----snipped--

</LinearLayout>

</LinearLayout>

</ScrollView>

Figure 8-2 depicts the Android screen corresponding to the preceding layout code.

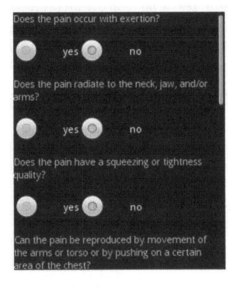

Figure 8-2. *Generated Android screen*

An XML file is automatically generated using, with results as follows:

```xml
<rules rule-name="chestpain">
<conditions name="EKG">
<or>
            <condition name="Is severe palmar pallor present?" value="yes">
</condition>
<condition name="Does the pain radiate to the neck, jaw, and/or arms?" value="yes">
</condition>
<condition name="Does the pain have a squeezing or tightness quality?" value="yes">
</condition>
</or>
<decision name="decisionString" value="ECG">
</decision>
</conditions>

</rules>
```

Using the XML, a CLIPS rule is generated automatically. The code snippet that generates the CLIPS rule is as follows:

```java
public static  void write ()
{
        File file = new File( ruleName + ".clp");
        // if file does not exists, then create it
System.out.println("Writing rule file ...");
        try {
        file.createNewFile();
        FileWriter fw = new FileWriter(file.getAbsoluteFile());
        BufferedWriter out = new BufferedWriter(fw);
        out.write("(defglobal ?*"+ ruleName +"DecisionString* = (create$))");
        out.write("(deftemplate " + ruleName +"_message\n\t(slot "+
decisionName[0] +")\n)");
        out.write("(deftemplate " + ruleName +"_data\n")
        List<String> uniqueVars=new ArrayList<String>();
        int ind=0;
    for(int j=0;j<cnlength;j++)
    {
        for(int i=0;i<gdlnQuestions[j].length;i++)
        {
            if(!uniqueVars.contains(varNamesArr[j][i]))
            {
                uniqueVars.add(ind, varNamesArr[j][i]);
                if(!gdlnQuestions[j][i].equals("null")) {
                    out.write("(slot "+varNamesArr[j][i] + ")\n");
                }
            }
        }
    }
    out.write(")\n\n");
    out.write("(defrule print_message_" + ruleName + "\n");
    out.write("\t("+ruleName+"_message("+decisionName[0]+" ?a))\n" );
```

```
                    out.write(" =>\n\t(bind ?*"+ ruleName +"DecisionString* (create$ ?*"+ ruleName
  +"DecisionString* ?a))\n)\n\n");

                    for(int j=0;j<cnlength;j++)
                    {
                            out.write("(defrule " + ruleName + "_" + conditionsName[j] + "\n");

                            if(isOrPresent[j] == true) {
                                    out.write("(or\n");
                            }
                            for(int i=0;i<gdlnQuestions[j].length;i++)
                            {
                                    if(!gdlnQuestions[j][i].equals("null")) {

                                    out.write("(" + ruleName +"_data("+varNamesArr[j][i] + " "
                                                    + anStrings[j][i] + "))\n" );
                                    }
                            }

                            if(isOrPresent[j] == true) {
                            out.write(")\n");
                            }
                            out.write("=>\n (assert ("+ ruleName +"_message(" + decisionName[j] + "
  \"" + decisionValue[j] + "\"))))\n\n");
                    }

                    out.close();
                    System.out.println("Done");
                            }
```

CLIPS Rules File Corresponding to Knowledge

The reader is advised to go through the CLIPS basic programming guide to get a good grasp of CLIPS rules syntax [23].

```
(defglobal ?*Chief_Complaint__Chest_Pain_DecisionString* =
(create$))
(deftemplate Chief_Complaint__Chest_Pain_message
        (slot decisionString)
)
(deftemplate Chief_Complaint__Chest_Pain_data
        (slot pain_exertion)
        (slot pain_radiate_neck_jaw_arms)
        (slot pain_squeezing_tightness_quality)
```

```
       (slot it_accompanied_shortness_breath_sweating_feeling_
       clamminess_nausea_indigestion)
       (slot If_pain_anginal_nature_it_last_more_than_15_30_
       minutes)
       (slot Can_pain_be_reproduced_movement_arms_torso_
       pushing_certain_area_chest)
       (slot pain_made_worse_deep_breathing)
       (slot pain_brought_eating_lying_down_it_relieved_
       antacids)
)
(defrule print_message_Chief_Complaint__Chest_Pain
       (Chief_Complaint__Chest_Pain_message(decisionString ?a))
  =>
       (bind ?*Chief_Complaint__Chest_Pain_DecisionString*
       (create$ ?*Chief_Complaint__Chest_Pain_DecisionString*
       ?a))
)
(defrule Chief_Complaint__Chest_Pain_EKG
(or
(Chief_Complaint__Chest_Pain_data(pain_exertion yes))
(Chief_Complaint__Chest_Pain_data(pain_radiate_neck_jaw_arms yes))
(Chief_Complaint__Chest_Pain_data(pain_squeezing_tightness_
quality yes))
(Chief_Complaint__Chest_Pain_data(it_accompanied_shortness_
breath_sweating_feeling_clamminess_nausea_indigestion yes))
(Chief_Complaint__Chest_Pain_data(If_pain_anginal_nature_it_
last_more_than_15_30_minutes yes))
)
=>
(assert (Chief_Complaint__Chest_Pain_message(decisionString
"EKG")))
)
```

```
(defrule Chief_Complaint__Chest_Pain_No_Test
(Chief_Complaint__Chest_Pain_data(pain_exertion no))
(Chief_Complaint__Chest_Pain_data(pain_radiate_neck_jaw_arms no))
(Chief_Complaint__Chest_Pain_data(pain_squeezing_tightness_
quality no))
(Chief_Complaint__Chest_Pain_data(Can_pain_be_reproduced_
movement_arms_torso_pushing_certain_area_chest no))
(Chief_Complaint__Chest_Pain_data(pain_made_worse_deep_
breathing no))
(Chief_Complaint__Chest_Pain_data(pain_brought_eating_lying_
down_it_relieved_antacids yes))
(Chief_Complaint__Chest_Pain_data(it_accompanied_shortness_
breath_sweating_feeling_clamminess_nausea_indigestion no))
(Chief_Complaint__Chest_Pain_data(If_pain_anginal_nature_it_
last_more_than_15_30_minutes no))
=>
(assert (Chief_Complaint__Chest_Pain_message(decisionString
"No Test")))
)
(defrule Chief_Complaint__Chest_Pain_chest_x-ray
(or
(Chief_Complaint__Chest_Pain_data(Can_pain_be_reproduced_
movement_arms_torso_pushing_certain_area_chest yes))
(Chief_Complaint__Chest_Pain_data(pain_made_worse_deep_
breathing yes))
)
=>
(assert (Chief_Complaint__Chest_Pain_message(decisionString
"chest x-ray")))
)
```

Knowledge Processing by Application

When the user selects the "chest pain" guideline in the knowledge application, a set of questions is presented (Figure 8-2). When the user answers the questions, a context manager constructs a CLIPS `assert` string and asserts it to the rules engine. The generated CLIPS rules files are already loaded into the rules engine at the time of application startup. The rules engine comes up with the result based on the rules files and user input. The context manager then reads the result back from the rules engine and sends it to the main activity for display.

Knowledge Application Supporting-Feature Generation

From the information present in the registration and settings files (Figures 8-3 and 8-4), SmartAppGen automatically generates a corresponding Android layout and activity file for the application.

registration	reg1			
field-text	field-type	field-subType	field-value	default-value
Patient's Age:	EditText	numeric	""	
Patient's Weight:	EditText	numeric	""	
Select Gender	Spinner		Prefer not to say:Male:Female	Prefer not to say
Area Name:	EditText	text	""	
Pin Code:	EditText	Numeric	""	

Figure 8-3. *User registration information*

settings	MainSetting					
field-text	field-type	field-input	field-value	default-v:	field-editabl	field-maxlength
Server IP	EditText	Phone		Default		10
Select Language	Spinner		English:Hin	English		10
Language Selected	EditText				FALSE	10
Asha registration	EditText					10

Figure 8-4. *Knowledge management app settings*

Figures 8-5 and 8-6 show the generated app.

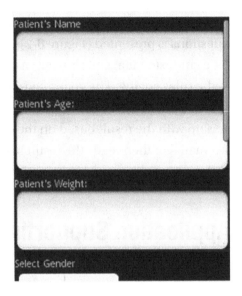

Figure 8-5. *Generated Registration screen*

Figure 8-6. *Generated Settings screen*

Generate Database Helper

SmartAppGen can also generate a database helper class automatically. The database helper class is required to persist application information. Database settings are depicted in Figure 8-7.

database	example1		woman:configuration:pk			
			field-name	field-type	field-null	
		woman	Id			
			id	varchar(60)	not null	
			Wname	varchar(40)	not null	
			Wage	int(2)	not null	
			update=WName:WAge, detail=WAge,WName:Weight prune=WAge<20			
		configuration	Component			
			Component	varchar(60)	not null	
			version	varchar(40)	not null	
			update=version	detail=version		

Figure 8-7. *Knowledge application database settings*

Here is a snippet of the generated database helper:

```
public class example1_DataHelper {
private static final String DATABASE_NAME = "example1";
private static final int DATABASE_VERSION = 4;
private static final String TABLE_REG1 = "reg1";
private Context context;
private SQLiteDatabase db;
public example1_DataHelper(Context context) {
this.context = context;
OpenHelper openHelper = new OpenHelper(this.context);
this.db = openHelper.getWritableDatabase();
}
public long insert_reg1(String values)
{
long returnValue = 1;
String executeString = "insert into " + TABLE_REG1 + " values
(" + values +");";
```

```java
Log.d("insert",executeString);
try {
db.execSQL(executeString);
}
catch(SQLiteException e) {
Log.e("Database error while inserting",e.toString());
returnValue = 0;
}
return returnValue;
}
public long update_reg1(String pk, String Age, String Weight,
String Gender, String Area, String Pincode)
{
long returnValue = 1;
String executeString = "update " + TABLE_REG1 + " set "+
"Age = '" + Age + "'," + "Weight = '" + Weight + "'," +
"Gender = '" + Gender + "'," + "Area = '" + Area + "'," +
"Pincode = '" + Pincode + "'"  + " where Id = '" + pk + "' ;";
Log.d("update",executeString);
try {
db.execSQL(executeString);
}
catch(SQLiteException e) {
Log.e("Database error while updating",e.toString());
returnValue = 0;
}
return returnValue;
}
public String getName_reg1(String pk)
{
String str = "";
```

```java
Cursor cursor = this.db.query (TABLE_REG1, new String[]
{"Name"}, "Id" + "="+"?", new String[]{pk}, null, null, "ID
desc");
if (cursor.moveToFirst())
{
str = cursor.getString(0);
}
if (cursor != null && !cursor.isClosed()) {
cursor.close();
}
return str;
}
public void deleteAll_reg1()
{
this.db.delete(TABLE_REG1, null, null);
}
public List<String> selectAll_reg1()
{
List<String>list = new ArrayList<String>();
Cursor cursor = this.db.query (TABLE_REG1, new String[]
{ "Id" }, null, null, null, null, "ID desc");
if (cursor.moveToFirst()) {
do {
list.add(cursor.getString(0));
} while (cursor.moveToNext());
}
if (cursor != null && !cursor.isClosed()) {
cursor.close();
}
return list;
}
```

```java
public void prune(String tableName, String condition)
{
String sql="delete from "+ tableName + " where " + condition;
db.rawQuery(sql, null).moveToFirst();
}
public void pruneAll(String[] tableName, String[] condition)
{
for(int i=0;i<tableName.length;i++){
prune(tableName[i],condition[i]);
}
}
private static class OpenHelper extends SQLiteOpenHelper {
OpenHelper(Context context) {
super(context, DATABASE_NAME, null, DATABASE_VERSION);
}@Override
public void onCreate(SQLiteDatabase db) {
try {
String execStr;
execStr = "CREATE TABLE " + TABLE_REG1 + " (Id varchar(60) not
null, Name varchar(60) not null, Age int(3) not null, Weight
int(3) not null, Gender varchar(60) not null, Area varchar(60)
not null, Pincode int(6) not null, PRIMARY KEY (Id) )";
Log.d("example1_DataHelper \n",execStr);
db.execSQL(execStr);
}catch(SQLiteException e) {
Log.e("Database error",e.toString());
}
}
@Override
public void onUpgrade(SQLiteDatabase db, int oldVersion, int
newVersion) {
```

```
Log.w("Example", "Upgrading database, this will drop tables and
recreate.");
db.execSQL("DROP TABLE IF EXISTS " + TABLE_REG1);
onCreate(db);
}
}
}
```

How to Use SmartAppGen

Create a new Android project and provide main Android layout, main activity Java file, AndroidManifest.xml, Excel sheet/text file containing knowledge, and application configuration as runtime argument to SmartAppGen and run it. All codes get generated and copied along with reusable frameworks developed as part of SmartAppGen to the Android project. Just refresh the project and do a clean build and run it. Your knowledge application is ready for deployment.

Benefits of SmartAppGen

The following benefits can easily be observed:

- The SmartAppGen accelerator frameworks will significantly reduce time to develop any knowledge applications by 30 to 50 percent.

- The generic frameworks (audio capturer, text to speech, photo capturer, upload manager, rules updater, etc.) can be reused in any Android project.

AutoQuiz: Automatically Generate Quiz from Unstructured Knowledge

In this chapter, we will show how to automatically build a quiz application from knowledge using natural language processing (NLP) techniques. NLP provides a way to process, understand, and derive meaning from human language. Apple's SIRI, Google's Home, Amazon's Echo, and Microsoft's Cortana are few examples of NLP systems.

To validate a user's learning from a training, he or she needs to undergo a test corresponding to the training material and score above a threshold decided by the company or institute.

One of the most time-consuming aspects of such testing is the generation of questions. They usually have to be constructed manually by experts in the subject. Furthermore, the validation of answers is time-consuming too, depending on the nature of the questions and the number of users.

© Chinmoy Mukherjee 2018
C. Mukherjee, *Build Android-Based Smart Applications*,
https://doi.org/10.1007/978-1-4842-3327-6_9

AutoQuiz solves this problem by automating the generation of questions. We extract the knowledge from the training materials and then validate the users' learning by presenting them with the quizzes.

AutoQuiz accepts text-based training material as input, which serves the purpose in most cases, since text can be easily extracted from various types of documents like PPT, PDF, Word doc, and so forth and fed into the AutoQuiz knowledge-management system.

The AutoQuiz system has two components: the question generator and the knowledge application that displays the quiz and the score of the user.

Question Generator

It takes a text-based article in a .txt file and outputs an XML file containing the questions, answers, options, and so forth. Upon initiating the program, the user enters the file name of article (including pathname if not in current directory). The program uses the Stanford NER (Named Entity Recognition) tagger to tag words of the following categories: Time, Location, Organization, Person, Money, Percent, and Date.

The program then uses the Stanford POS (Part of Speech) tagger [16], v.3.2.0, which is open source. It uses the API of the Penn Treebank tag set [20] to tag words according to their POS. It uses 60–200 MB to run a trained tagger with this API, which is fairly low compared to other taggers like OpenNLP [17], which uses about 3–4 GB to run, with the trainer provided by default. However, OpenNLP also provides other tools, like sentence segmentation and named entity extraction, which are not supported by the Stanford POS tagger but that would be useful to our application. After tagging the words, the tagged words are stored in a text file, from which each sentence is parsed and converted into one of four different types of questions:

- Keyword questions: These are "fill in the blank" questions where there are no options and the right answer is a keyword from the sentence. This keyword is a proper noun detected by the POS tagger. Generally, proper nouns are good keywords, because they are usually the subject of the sentence. An extension would be to use the OpenNLP tools to detect the head of the sentence and make that the keyword.

- Noun questions: This is another "fill in the blank" question where nouns are detected via the POS tagger but options are provided for the answer. Options are nouns from other sentences. A key factor in the quality of these questions is the sense and relevance of the questions and options. We plan to provide options with attributes and scan through the pool of all answers to look for the same attribute when selecting the options. For example:

  Input sentence:

- "An Engineer is trying to develop lightweight, 'air breathing' hypersonic vehicles that can travel at rocket-like speeds while taking oxygen from the atmosphere."

  Noun: engineer

  Attribute: profession

- We use WordNet [18] to find its siblings in a tree of professions; for example, scientist, electrician, technologist, and so forth.

- Investigative questions (first kind): These are questions that are of an investigative nature; for example:

Input sentence: "Jake was the one who took the car."

Question: "Who was the one who took the car?"

- These questions look for verbs in the third person, past tense. This is because most descriptive articles use sentences in the third person past tense. In addition, the answer must contain a proper noun to avoid trivial cases like: "It was lying on the table."

Without this rule, the answer would be "It," which is not a meaningful question.

"Who/what" questions can be refined to be either who or what (or even when, how much, and so forth) using named entity recognition software, for example, Stanford Named entity recognizer [21], or OpenNLP tools [17].

- Investigative questions (second kind): These questions are similar to investigative questions of the first kind. Instead of starting with the questioning words, they end with the questioning words. For example:

Input sentence: "Jake was the one who took the car."

Question: "Jake was the one who took the what?"

Similarly, a named entity recognizer can be used to refine the wording of the questions.

These questions are stored in an XML file under the following format:

```
<questions guideline-name=Quiz name>
<question>
        <question-text>question</question-text>
        <answer-type>RadioButton/Text</ answer-type>
```

```
        <answer-value>answer</answer-value>
        <option-value>option1:option2...</option-value>
</question>
<question>
```

This XML file is stored in the second project—the Android application project. The exact location is a user input to the first project. The field is encrypted using a simple variation of the Caesar cipher: in the ASCII table, all the characters are shifted by a certain index. This would prevent the visibility of the answer if a user decided to extract the files from the installed application.

Quiz Application

The application reads the XML files and creates a separate quiz for each file. The user can determine the number of questions per page. A progress bar indicates what fraction of the quiz has been completed. At the end, the user is given his or her score for that quiz. The screenshots in Figures 9-1 to 9-3 will help you better understand the application workflow.

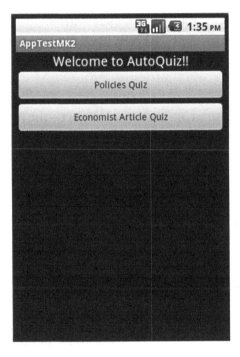

Figure 9-1. *AutoQuiz application*

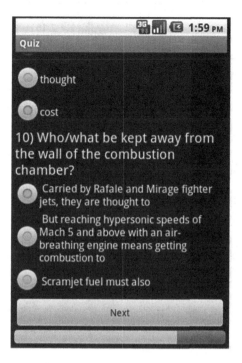

Figure 9-2. *Quiz questions*

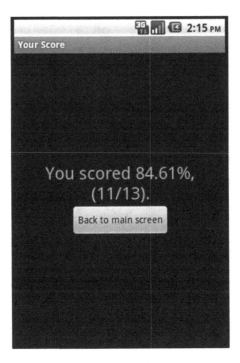

Figure 9-3. *Quiz score*

Benefits of AutoQuiz

We can easily observe the following benefits of the AutoQuiz system:

- Automatically generate quizzes based on training/ presentation materials, saving hours of effort to prepare quiz manually

- Automatically validate quiz answers, again saving hours of effort to validate answers manually

- Makes training/presentation more effective, as people attending training would have to answer quiz generated by AutoQuiz, and they and their manager get to know the score immediately

- Measure effectiveness of trainer and training materials

Known Issues

We still need to resolve the following issues for AutoQuiz system:

- In the "fill in the blanks" and "nouns" questions, the options may not always make sense, making it easy for the test taker to answer the question correctly without having knowledge of the article. We intend to tackle this problem by tagging the words in the options-pool with attributes.

- Investigative questions of both kinds can become too monotonous and robotic if they only use who/what. These are used because of AutoQuiz's inability to recognize the subject in the sentence.

- Focus of sentence: The current prototypes are unable to recognize the subject of the sentence and give more meaningful questions. For example:

  Input sentence: "Only the thief wears a black hat."

  Here, the focus is on "thief" and not, say, the color of the hat.

  Suitable question: "Who wears a black hat?"

  Less suitable question: "What color hat does the thief wear?"

- Extracting knowledge: The current prototypes only extract knowledge on a high level and not in detail. They do not use rules to store the knowledge, so they cannot be used to make derivations. For example:

Input:

"Joe is the brother of John. John is the brother of Jake."

Possible derivation: "Joe is a brother of Jake."

We present possible solutions to these issues in the next section.

Future Work

Named Entity Recognition software can be used to refine the "who/what" questions to be more specific. This would aid in adding clarity for the user and would also improve the quality of the questions. This data can be used to highly specialize questions; for example, who, what, when, how much, and so forth. Furthermore, it would also aid in recognizing the head of the sentence.

Another refinement that could be made is allowing the person creating the quiz to select the sentences for which to generate questions, rather than using every sentence. A key criterion could be the presence of words with a particular POS that is crucial to the question.

Furthermore, compound sentences could either be split into two separate sentences or be used as questions and answers. For example:

Input sentence:

"Joe went to the kitchen because he was hungry."

("Joe went to the kitchen.") + ("He was hungry.")

Possible questions:

"Who went to the kitchen?"

"Who was hungry?"

"Why did Joe go to the kitchen?" (Answer: "because he was hungry")

However, questions like these require a greater understanding of the sentences by the program. A first step would be to parse the sentence in such a way that we can recognize the head and the body of the sentence. The OpenNLP parser can be used to determine the structure of a sentence. For example:

Input sentence: "The quick brown fox jumps over the lazy dog."

Output:

```
(TOP
(NP
(NP
(DT The)
(JJ quick)
(JJ brown)
(NN fox)
(NNS jumps)
)
(PP
(IN over)
(NP
(DT the)
(JJ lazy)
 (NN dog)
)
)
(. .)
```

PP, IN, JJ, etc. are the POS tags from the Penn Treebank tagset [20]. Sentences parsed in this way can aid in computers' understanding of the structure of the sentence and help them generate questions that are more inventive than simply manipulating the original sentence.

Furthermore, sentences parsed in this way can aid in extracting the knowledge from the sentence. Knowledge can be stored in the form of rules (for example, CLIPS [19], which is a rules engine). These rules can act as predicates that can be used to derive conclusions. These conclusions will be stored as new rules, and they can also be output as questions.

Knowledge-management automation needs to be planned by corporates. "Knowledge application" can be automatically generated from the available structured knowledge. Such application can help knowledge workers perform their daily job better. This would significantly reduce the time needed to train people and increase the efficiency and accuracy of the knowledge workers.

When training employees on unstructured knowledge, companies continue to spend millions of dollars; many of the trainings are not effective and waste those dollars. Implementing AutoQuiz can ensure that employees actually understand the knowledge shared in a training or presentation. Project managers can assess the effectiveness of the training or presentation (for example, which training is redundant, which employee is a slow learner, which trainer is not effective, and so forth) and take appropriate action.

CHAPTER 10

iEmergency

In most of the developing world, if a person faces an emergency situation—like getting mugged, being beaten, getting molested, getting lost in an unknown place, meeting with an accident, needing a safety guide, and so on—there is hardly any help available. The longer the person stays in the emergency situation, the more the probability of losing life or belongings increases. In countries like India, the ratio of people to police personnel is 125:100000, and the roads are heavily congested with traffic during peak hours. Hence, most of the time police are unable to attend to the crime quickly. It generally takes more than two hours for the police to reach the crime scene! Also, it has been observed that the common public is either not interested or too afraid to provide emergency help to the needy, fearing attack by the culprits. This results in major physical, emotional, and economical damage to the victim, and may even lead to death.

The proposed system, iEmergency, aims to provide on-the-spot emergency help to victims via a network of registered emergency help providers. The victim can initiate a request for emergency help using their smartphone. The mobile network finds nearby emergency help providers using location-based services and notifies them. Emergency help providers reach out to the victim and provide required assistance. On completion of the help to the satisfaction of the victim, a fixed amount of money is deducted from the victim's account and distributed among the emergency help providers who responded to the request and provided help on the spot within the specified timeframe.

© Chinmoy Mukherjee 2018
C. Mukherjee, *Build Android-Based Smart Applications*,
https://doi.org/10.1007/978-1-4842-3327-6_10

Method

When a person is facing an emergency situation, he or she can initiate a request for emergency help using the application installed in his or her smartphone. The requester needs to choose the type of emergency help required. The emergency situation details along with the requester's location (e.g., GPS/GPRS) are uploaded to the iEmergency server. A person can select and register for various types of emergency services depending upon his or her capabilities. For example, a person residing near a highway can register as an accident relief service provider, retired military or police personnel can register themselves as petty crime-prevention service providers, social service-minded persons can register as companions for hospital trips, and so forth. The server identifies the emergency helper(s) available within a specified radius from the location of the requester who match the type of help that he or she is looking for. The server determines the number of emergency helpers required for the type of emergency faced by the person and sends details about the emergency and the requester (name, location, and photo) to the emergency helper(s). Emergency helper(s) receive a message such as "Mr. <name> <mobile number> is facing emergency situation of type <type> at <location>." The emergency helper can visualize the requester's current position on the map. The emergency helper(s) can either accept or reject the service request.

If an emergency helper accepts the request, he or she can retrieve the audio/video file(s) associated with the requester and gather more information about their location and type of emergency. The requester side of the application has the ability to upload audio or video files. He or she may record an emergency message and upload the audio to the server so it can be downloaded by the helper. The emergency helper tries to come as near as possible to the requester's location and either shouts the name of the person or calls him or her using the mobile phone. The server periodically receives location details of the available emergency helper(s) so that, in case of any emergency event, the server knows their location.

Architecture

The architecture of the proposed system with a high-level work flow is illustrated in Figure 10-1. The system consists of Requester and Helper applications and a centralized server. The requester sends a request for emergency service by starting the Requester application installed on his or her Smartphone. The application sends a request to the server to send helpers to the spot. The server notifies nearby helpers about the emergency. The helpers reach the spot and provide requester with required service. The requester then proceeds to pay the helpers. The server responds back with the list of helpers who had accepted the request. The requester identifies the helpers from the list to select the helpers who actually came to help, and the requester pays those helpers (Figure 10-6). The payment server authenticates the requester and sends payment to the helper.

The Helper application scans for requests from nearby requesters. The server retrieves details of the person waiting for help in the vicinity of the helper and sends the details in response. The Helper application displays the requester as well as helper on a map. The helper accepts or rejects the request. The helper helps the requester and, after receiving the payment notification, he or she marks the job complete and provides feedback (Figure 10-7).

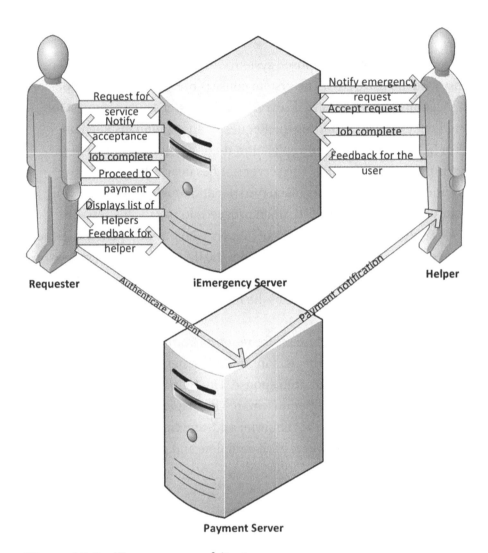

Figure 10-1. *iEmergency architecture*

Implementation of the System

The system consists of Requester (iRescue) and Helper (iRescuer) Android applications, used by the requester and helpers respectively, and a centralized server. Any individual can register on the portal as a requester and/or a helper. At the time of registration, the person has to provide details such as mobile number that will be used for the service, recent photograph, and email ID as well as upload copies of identity and address proof. The submitted information will be verified either automatically (mobile number and email ID) or manually (address) to ensure that the helpers are genuine persons. Help from law enforcement authorities may be sought for manual verification of the helpers.

Requester Application iRescue

This application is installed on the requester's mobile phone. When he or she faces an emergency situation, he or she starts the application, enters a PIN, and records his or her voice to provide more details about the emergency faced. Details of the emergency situation and related audio or any media file(s) are uploaded to a central server HTTP POST request. In addition to that, when the server finds that a helper associated with the requester has reached within an audible distance, the application starts beeping loudly. When the helper reaches the person and provides the required emergency service, the application retrieves the list of helpers who had accepted the request and displays it to requester. The photo, name, and mobile number of the helpers are displayed in the application. The requester can choose one or more helpers from the list and authenticate payment. Feedback can also be left for the helpers. The feedback for the helpers is uploaded to the server.

Helper Application iRescuer

This application is installed on the helper's mobile phone. By using location-based services (LBS), it periodically sends the helper's location information to the server. It retrieves details of the nearest requester waiting to receive emergency help. It shows the helper as well as the requester on a map. It also displays the current distance of the requester from the helper. The helper can either accept or reject the request. If the request is rejected, the server updates the record of helper. If the helper decides to accept the request, further details of the person in need (name, mobile number, and photo) are displayed. The helper can also download any audio associated with the requester and play it to gather additional information about the emergency.

Once the helper reaches the requester, provides emergency service, and receives payment, he or she marks the job as complete in the application and provides feedback on the requester.

User Interface

Some of the main screens of the iRescue and iRescuer applications have been depicted in Figures 10-2 to 10-7, which display the different type of emergencies that the iEmergency system supports. As an example, Figure 10-5 displays a map where both helper and victim are plotted. Figure 10-6 displays a photo of the requester, and Figure 10-7 displays photo and details of helpers who actually provided the service.

Figure 10-2. *iRescue type of emergency*

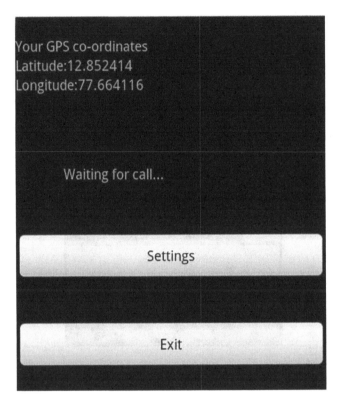

Figure 10-3. *iRescuer waiting*

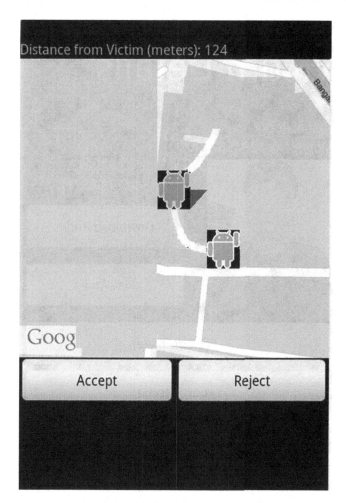

Figure 10-4. *iRescuer accept/reject*

Figure 10-5. *iRescuer victim details*

Figure 10-6. iRescue payment

Figure 10-7. *iRescuer job complete*

iEmergency Server

The iEmergency server is built on top of the Apache XAMPP platform. It consists of one Apache server and one MySQL server. The server receives various requests from helper(s) and requester(s) via HTTP POST and HTTP GET and sends HTTP responses to both iRescue and iRescuer applications. It maintains various details of registered requester(s) and helper(s). The server sends nearby victim details to the iRescuer application. It also stores audio details of the requester and allows the helper to download the audio. In addition to that, feedback for the transaction between requester and helper is recorded in the server.

PART III

Android Applications for Solving Real-Life Problems

CHAPTER 11

Assignments

This chapter contains multiple assignments that will test what you have learned from previous chapter.

iEncrypt and iDecrypt

Come up with two android applications—say, iEncrypt and iDecrypt. iEncrypt will take a password and image file to encrypt and the type of context/rule to be added while encrypting.

The following screenshots (Figures 11-1 to 11-5) will help you understand the application requirements.

117

© Chinmoy Mukherjee 2018
C. Mukherjee, *Build Android-Based Smart Applications*,
https://doi.org/10.1007/978-1-4842-3327-6_11

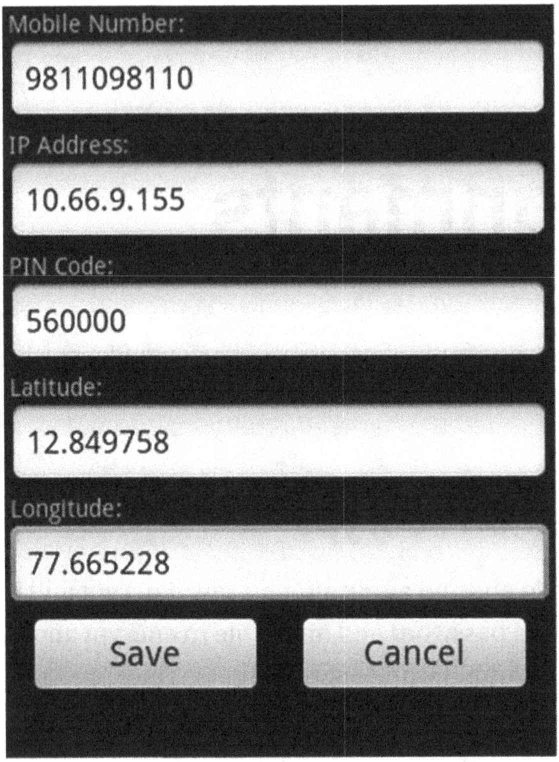

Figure 11-1. *iEncrypt setting*

Figure 11-2. *iEncrypt input*

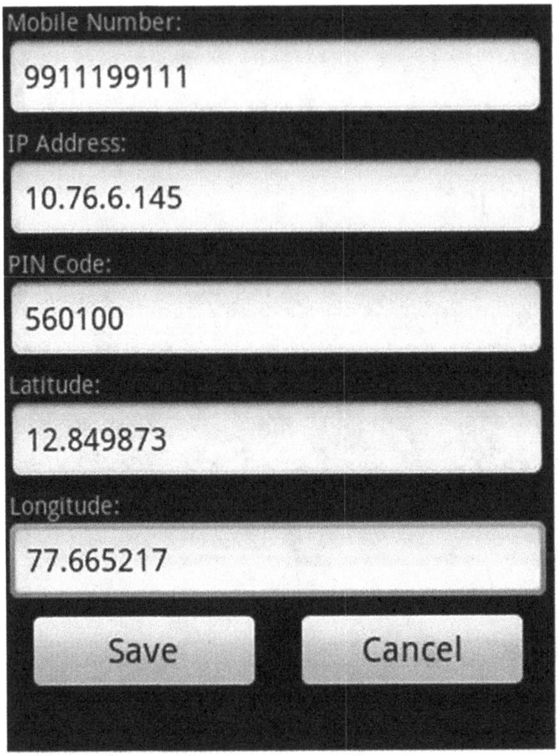

Figure 11-3. iDecrypt setting

Figure 11-4. *iDecrypt input*

Figure 11-5. *iDecrypt decrypted content*

iFitness

Many times, when a user is exercising—for example, running on a treadmill—he or she either runs too slow or runs too fast, making the workout ineffective or harmful.

Develop an Android application to help the user measure the effectiveness of his or her fitness program. Let the user wear a strap (Figure 11-6) that transmits vital parameters, like number of steps, speed, heart rate, and so forth, to an Android application over Bluetooth. Configure the exercise mode as depicted in Figure 11-7).

122

Figure 11-6. *Zephyr strap*

Figure 11-7. *iFitness main screen*

In the settings, configure upper and lower thresholds of speed for each of the categories. For example, "FAT BURN" speed can be between 10 and 20 km/hour. Also define what is considered the "above normal" threshold for heart rate. In addition to that, advise the user based on his or her speed and selected exercise mode. Also, advise the user to stop exercising immediately if his or her heart rate crosses the upper threshold defined.

iPocket

The pick-pocketing of mobile phones is a huge menace in developing countries, and even developed countries like Spain, Italy, and France are severely affected by it. Millions of mobile phones are lost every year due to pick-pocketing. How can we detect a phone getting pick-pocketed in real-time?

When someone pick-pockets a phone, the accelerometer data pattern is significantly different than that of the pattern that occurs when a person picks his/her phone from pocket for making/receiving calls. Develop an Android service to monitor the accelerometer pattern. Identify the pick-pocketing pattern by collecting 10–12 data points any time phone is picked up and comparing the accelerometer data with the normal as well as the pick-pocketing data points.

iFall

Elderly people often fall down, and it can happen while they are home alone; they can even fall unconscious following the fall. Can an Android application detect such emergencies and inform a concerned emergency contact?

Collect 10–12 accelerometer readings when a person falls down with a phone inside his or her pocket as well as in his or her hand. Run a service in the phone to check for such accelerometer patterns. When a similar pattern is detected, wake up the iFall Android application and ask the user, "Are you Okay?" If the user says yes, the application exits; otherwise, the application retries to get a response from user. If no response is received, the app sends a text message with location, time details, and a message like "User seems to have fallen down, not responding for past X minutes" to preconfigured mobile numbers. The mobile numbers must be configured using the settings of the iFall application.

iPrescribe

Patients often forget to take medicine on time. Also, once the symptoms subside, patients stop taking their medicines altogether, due to which they do not recover completely and may fall sick again.

Feed the prescription along with the dosing schedule into the iPrescribe application. Remind the user, saying things like, "It's 9 p.m., please take 1 crocin tablet, and also take 1 teaspoon of zedex syrup at five past 9 p.m." After a configurable number of minutes, the application will ask the patient, "Did you take medicines as prescribed?" The patient can answer "yes" or "no"; if the patient says "no," iPrescribe will ask them the reason for not taking the medicine, then it records the reason and stores it along with the prescription schedule.

At the end of the schedule, the data can be uploaded to a central server and analyzed for studying the effectiveness of the medicines prescribed. iPrescribe should also be able to come up with a health negligence quotient for the patient based on how religiously they followed the prescription schedule.

Think about whether prescriptions could be fed into the iPrescribe Android application automatically.

iSafety

In developing countries, crimes against children (on the way to school/home) have increased significantly in recent years. How can we ensure the safety of kids and family when they are out from sight?

Develop a safe-zone application and install it on the child's phone. Configure safe zones, like school, home, and so forth. If the person happens to stay out of a safe zone for more than a configurable number of minutes, start sending SMS along with GPS location details of the person periodically. The person receiving the SMS and location details can plot the locations in a map and determine a further course of action.

In this chapter, we learned how to design and develop a complete system using Android applications and a backend server to solve real-life problems. We also hope that after going through the problems, readers will be able to come up with new Android project ideas.

References

1. John R. Rymer and Mike Gualtieri, "Market Overview: Business Rules Platforms 2011," July 5, 2011. Available at: `http://www.forrester.com/Market+Overview+Business+Rules+Platforms+2011/fulltext/-/E-RES58570?aid=AST152422`.

2. "World Mobile Applications Market Worth US$25 Billion by 2015", Press Release. Available at: `http://www.marketsandmarkets.com/PressReleases/mobile-applications-market.asp`.

3. "10 Cutting-Edge Mobile Application Trends for 2012," *ItBusinessEdge.com*. Available at: `http://www.itbusinessedge.com/slideshows/show.aspx?c=87261`.

4. `http://www.android.com/`

5. Heather Leonard, "So, Who Is Winning—iOS or Android?" *Business Insider*, April 18, 2013. Available at: `http://www.businessinsider.com/so-who-is-winning-ios-or-android-2013-44`.

6. `http://clipsrules.sourceforge.net/`

7. `http://jruleengine.sourceforge.net/`

8. `http://dtrules.com/`

9. `http://sourceforge.net/projects/zilonis`

127

© Chinmoy Mukherjee 2018
C. Mukherjee, *Build Android-Based Smart Applications*,
https://doi.org/10.1007/978-1-4842-3327-6

10. http://www.gradsoft.ua/products/termware_
    eng.html

11. http://roolie.sourceforge.net/

12. http://openrules.com/

13. http://sourceforge.net/projects/jxbre/

14. http://www.cin.ufpe.br/jeops/

15. https://github.com/commonsguy/cwac-updater

16. The Stanford Natural Language Processing Group,
    "Stanford Log-linear Part-Of-Speech Tagger,"
    available at: http://nlp.stanford.edu/software/
    tagger.shtml.

17. OpenNLP software tools: http://wordnet.
    princeton.edu/

18. Princeton University, "WordNet: A Lexical Database
    for English," available at: http://wordnet.
    princeton.edu/.

19. "CLIPS: A Tool for Building Expert Systems,"
    available at: http://clipsrules.sourceforge.
    net/.

20. Penn Treebak tagset: http://www.mozart-oz.org/
    mogul/doc/lager/brill-tagger/penn.html

21. The Stanford Natural Language Processing Group,
    "Stanford Named Entity Recognizer (NER),"
    available at: http://nlp.stanford.edu/software/
    CRF-NER.shtml.

22. "Rete Algorithm," https://en.wikipedia.org/
    wiki/Rete_algorithm.

23. "CLIPS Reference Manual, Volume 1: Basic Programming Guide," version 6.30, March 17, 2015. Available at: http://clipsrules.sourceforge. net/documentation/v630/bpg.pdf.

24. https://sourceforge.net/projects/clipsrules/ files/CLIPS/6.30/clips_jni_050.zip/download

25. "Knowledge Management," https://en.wikipedia. org/wiki/Knowledge_management.

Index

131

© Chinmoy Mukherjee 2018
C. Mukherjee, *Build Android-Based Smart Applications*,
https://doi.org/10.1007/978-1-4842-3327-6

Get the eBook for only $5!

Why limit yourself?

With most of our titles available in both PDF and ePUB format, you can access your content wherever and however you wish—on your PC, phone, tablet, or reader.

Since you've purchased this print book, we are happy to offer you the eBook for just $5.

To learn more, go to http://www.apress.com/companion or contact support@apress.com.

Apress®

Printed in the United States
By Bookmasters